Wakefield Press

SILENT WITNESSES

Simon Cameron is a general practitioner who lives with his wife and three children in Glenelg, South Australia's historical heartland. He developed a passion for history from watching too many movies as a child, and became obsessed by it when he began reading all things historical. He realises that history rules our every move, and that understanding it is our only hope.

T0358159

SILENT WITNESSES

ADELAIDE'S STATUES AND MONUMENTS

Simon Cameron

Wakefield Press

Wakefield Press
Box 2266
Kent Town
South Australia 5071

First published 1997

Designed and typeset by Clinton Ellicott, MoBros, Adelaide
Printed and bound by Hyde Park Press, Adelaide

National Library of Australia
Cataloguing-in-publication entry

Cameron, Simon.
Silent witnesses: history of Adelaide's statues and monuments.
Includes index.
ISBN 1 86254 402 6.
1. Statues – South Australia – Adelaide – History.
2. Monuments – South Australia – Adelaide – History. I. Title.

731.760994231

Front cover photo: detail of South Australian National War Memorial, Spirit of Duty.
Back cover photo: Sir Ross Smith Memorial – panel showing arrival in Adelaide.

This publication was supported by the South Australian
Government through the State History Centre, a Division
of the History Trust of South Australia, and financially
supported by the Adelaide City Council.

CONTENTS

P R E F A C E

Statues and monuments fill streets and museums all over the world. The idea of skilful craftsmen and artists stamping their ideals in stone and bronze is as old as civilisation. Every monument tells a tale, not only of its subject but of the society that erects it. The ancient Egyptians were the first monumental stone craftsmen, erecting the largest stone memorials ever built. Theirs were monuments to the glory of their culture, dedicated to the gods and the afterlife, but also emphasising the power and wealth of the subject or donor. Lifelike representations meant nothing to ancient civilisations until the Greeks began to question the mythical and observe the natural. The Classical Greeks sought to glorify perfection, but their temples and votive offerings celebrated wealth, power and success just like the Egyptians. It is testament to the legacy of Greek thought and culture that bronze and stone memorials are still the symbols of success.

Most of Adelaide's statues were erected between 1892 and 1942, with 25 major works completed in this period. During the next 50 years there were only 11 minor works erected, including the busts that line North Terrace. This disparity is partly explained by the fall from fashion of the classical sculpture, which meant less enthusiasm for full-figure bronzes raised on pedestals. The earlier activity was also prompted by the desire to raise the cultural status of the young city.

The city fathers cherished the uniqueness of Adelaide's parks and boulevards and wanted to fill them with noble statues, mimicking the old cities of Europe. They chose classical gods and goddesses, monarchs, explorers and themselves as suitable subjects. This reflects the passions and interests of the period and explains the striking paucity of female recipients. Men controlled the fund-raising, and donations would usually come from wealthy businessmen who saw their contribution as a way to enhance their prestige and status. Statues were often planned and promoted in the close confines of the Adelaide Club. Funds for other monuments such as war memorials and royal statues were raised by public subscriptions, and their unveiling ceremonies were celebrated by huge crowds at lavish formal presentations.

All cities celebrate explorers and founders but Adelaide was a carefully planned business venture and heroes were few. Colonel Light, Charles Sturt, John McDouall Stuart and Matthew Flinders were all graced with statues but these were plagued by indifference and a lack of funds.

Since the 1960s large public subscriptions have disappeared and monuments have become less ambitious, often taking the form of a bust or plaque. These are usually erected by small interest groups or associations, and attract little public attention or celebration. It would be hard to imagine the populace of today agreeing on a subject worthy of a $700 000 memorial such as that created for Edward VII. Such noble visions have faded and the flood of statues has dried.

However, the monuments that stand tall in the City of Adelaide hold an important legacy from the past and are worthy of our care and attention.

I began my search for Adelaide's monuments in 1987, and quickly discovered that I would have to limit its scope to the city square and adjacent parklands. I have had to exclude the plethora of plaques that enliven our streets and choose the most substantial monuments. Even over this space of time new memorials have appeared, some have even disappeared, so at best I have been able to capture only a snapshot of Adelaide's statues and monuments.

Particular characters reappear throughout the history of Adelaide's statues and I have included brief biographies for as many as possible, usually where they first appear in the narrative. I have not repeated the biography each time, so the reader will have to refer to the index.

Comparing the monetary values of today with those of yesteryear is always difficult, but some rudimentary comparison can be given by looking at basic wage judgements periodically made by the South Australian Industrial Commission. I include the following rough guide for those interested in trying to equate the funds spent on Adelaide's statues with the values of today. Of course, Adelaide's statues are irreplaceable treasures, with artistic 'collectable' values which have far outstripped the rate of inflation.

1900	£1 = $230
1910	£1 = $200
1920	£1 = $125
1930	£1 = $105

AUTHOR'S NOTE

I thank the fates for granting an endless supply of enthusiastic, hard-working librarians and archivists, particularly in the Adelaide City Council Archives and the Mortlock Library of South Australiana. I also thank the Adelaide City Council and the State History Trust. I am indebted to Patricia Sumerling and Beverley Burke for their help and advice. To Jennifer and all those other proof-readers – what can I say, except promise not to do it again.

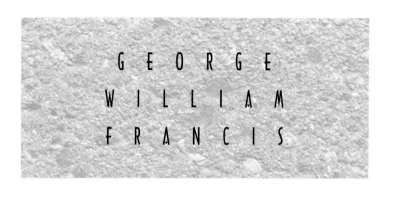

GEORGE
WILLIAM
FRANCIS

Botanic Gardens, 30 metres north-east of the main entrance

Two metres tall white obelisk enclosed on three sides by shrubs. A central bronze plaque states: 'In remembrance of the late GW Francis Esq, FLS FHS. First director of this garden by whom it was planned and laid out in the year 1855.' Unveiled 28 May 1866.

Adelaide's earliest surviving public monument is a humble white obelisk commemorating a gentleman colonist who achieved his dream of establishing a botanic garden. In only ten years, and despite miserly government support, he singlemindedly transformed a soggy patch of parkland into a thriving popular attraction. It was a labour of love.

George William Francis migrated to Adelaide with his wife and six children in 1849, when the colony of South Australia was just emerging from its first economic crisis. A well educated man, he had unique skills to offer and quickly became involved in various societies and organisations, including the South Australian Library and Mechanics'

Institute. He also joined the committee of the Floricultural and Horticultural Society.

Francis's botanical credentials were impressive. Although self-taught, he had become an expert on English flora, publishing monographs and lecturing to the public and fellow enthusiasts. He was made a Fellow of the Linnean Society in 1839, but had failed to secure an academic or curatorial post in Britain. It is clear that he came to South Australia determined to establish a botanical garden, since he immediately made submissions to Governor Young to do so. There had already been attempts to establish a public garden in the infant colony beside the Adelaide gaol, and it may have been news of the failure of these ventures that had brought Francis to the plains of Adelaide.

The vacant site of the old Botanic Gardens was leased to Francis but no government funding was forthcoming. It took six years of patient lobbying and planning before financial support was granted. Francis submitted his plans and pre-ferred site to the government in 1851 and in 1855 defended his choice in a detailed report and estimates which became the blueprint for the Botanic Gardens. With a grant of £600 he at last began planting in June 1855 and, remarkably, he was able to open the garden to the public within two years.

The garden was an immediate public success, even in those early days of construction, drainage, ponding and planting. More than just a showcase, it was developed as a horticultural resource, testing and distributing seed stock for the colony. He established contact with other botanical gardens throughout the Empire and provided information to all and sundry. Within ten years, up to his death in 1865, this energetic man was able to establish a professional garden, complete with glasshouses, conservatories and rambling walks, which was treasured by the citizens of Adelaide. Although he is largely forgotten today, his legacy is enjoyed by thousands.

References
Best, B *George William Francis*, Adelaide, 1986
Register, 26 August 1865, p 4

FIREMAN GARDNER'S MEMORIAL

Elder Park, King William Road

Wrought iron fountain sheltered by a marble cupola supported by four columns. The spout is formed by a rather heavily browed face. Four hitching posts guard the front, and shields and wreaths decorate the four sides, inscribed with the words 'Fireman Gardner's Memorial 1887'. A small bronze plaque at the base records that 'this drinking fountain commemorates the heroism of Fireman John Gardner who died fighting a fire of large dimension in Rundle Street near James Place on Christmas Eve 1886'. Unveiled 10 October 1887.

Fireman Gardner's functional memorial, erected in recognition of a simple man's misfortune and sacrifice, is today an elegant Victorian decoration in the most Victorian of Adelaide's public parks. Its brief inscription does not tell the full tale of the tragic Christmas Eve in 1886 when excited late night shoppers in Rundle Street were startled by flames pouring from Castle's drapery store, close to Gays Arcade. As the gas lamps were lit, the overcrowded draper's window, festooned with brocades and lace, had caught fire. With a delay of 20 minutes before the fire brigade arrived, the fire had spread to the adjoining Cunningham's fancy goods store and the luckless Academy of Music, an entertainment hall that had been burnt twice before.

Firemen John Gardner and Albert Clark had barely hauled the fire hose 15 feet into Cunningham's store before the ceiling collapsed. Gardner disappeared, engulfed in the burning debris, and Clark was pulled badly burnt from beneath the fallen timbers. Gardner's body was not found until the early hours of Christmas morning and Clark died on the same day in the Adelaide Hospital.

The subsequent inquest resulted in a number of improvements to the city's fire safety. The slow response of the brigade led to the installation of fire alarms on city streets and the poor water pressure, which had been exacerbated by the hot dry summer, led to the purchase of a steam-driven engine and pump. The inquest also highlighted poor building standards, in particular the erection of wide buildings with insufficient spanning beams to support the upper floors.

Fireman Gardner's memorial stands in the public parklands, but it was the desire to erect a private monument to Albert Clark that triggered the Gardner appeal. Clark was a well known local sportsman and his family and friends immediately started a collection to raise a memorial. In contrast, John Gardner, a 'new chum' and a single man, had arrived in the colony only two years before. The public quickly took up his cause, and in letters to the press pleaded for a combined memorial. Clark's family declined and, wishing to keep their monument personal and private, placed it over his grave in the North Road cemetery, where it still

stands in a lapsed plot which may one day make way for a
new owner.

With the Clark family holding their private service,
Gardner became the sole focus of a public that was gripped
by a sense of tragedy and selfless duty. After a public funeral
service he was buried at the Mitcham cemetery, and a committee collected over £160 for the erection of his memorial.
The committee chose a public drinking fountain, which was
designed and carved by F Herring, and a monument was
also raised over his grave. The *Register* reports that a full-
length painting of Gardner was donated to the fire brigade,
but no trace of such a memorial can be found.

The drinking fountain was formally given to the City of
Adelaide on 10 October 1887 and accepted by the Mayor,
Edwin Thomas Smith. For over a century the City Council
has faithfully maintained the memorial and it still gushes
freely. It sits easily amid the trees lining the busy thoroughfare, so unobtrusively that few notice it.

John Gardner's death was ennobled by his role as a
fireman, with his memorial symbolising duty and sacrifice.
The tragedy also deserves to be remembered as the tragic
death of two young men amidst the celebrations of Christmas.

References
Observer, 15 October 1887, p 33

Register, 27 December 1886, p 6; 27 January 1887, p 7;
    5 April 1887, p 5; 1 July 1887, p 5; 19 January 1887, p 5

VENERE DI CANOVA

(CANOVA'S VENUS)

Prince Henry Gardens, between King William Street and Kintore Avenue, North Terrace

Life-size white Carrara marble standing on a base of Sicilian marble and elevated on a pedestal of Kapunda stone. The words 'Venere di Canova' are carved on the edge of the Sicilian base. A faded inscription on top of the pedestal is just discernible as 'Brothers Pugi Florence'. An inscription on the pedestal states that the Venus 'was presented to the Corporation of Adelaide 1892 by WA Horn'. Unveiled 3 September 1892.

Canova's Venus holds the honour of being Adelaide's first street statue, and it was intended to be a refining influence on a community preoccupied with commerce. The donor, William Austin Horn had already made his fortune and could therefore afford to be self-righteous. Explorer, pastoralist, mining magnate and philanthropist, Horn's interests were as eclectic as his nature was restless. Although city raised, he became a keen explorer and a skilled bushman,

learning local Aboriginal dialects. He developed his skills while searching for grazing lands and his tenacity ensured his success as a pastoralist. Another facet of his personality was displayed when, during his first finance-raising trip to London in 1872, he took the opportunity to study Classics at Oxford University.

Horn owned pastoral properties adjoining Silverton and he became a founding shareholder of BHP, which assured his life-long financial security. During the rural set-back in South Australia of 1880 he gained great public esteem for his generous financial support of his constituents. In 1887 he entered the South Australian legislature as an independent, remaining a satirical thorn in the side of successive governments until his retirement from politics in 1893 to write and sculpt. In 1894 he funded a scientific expedition to the MacDonnell Ranges. His restlessness continued and he travelled frequently, to Europe, New Zealand and throughout Australia. His sojourns in the outback kept him from home for weeks on end, yet despite his love of the bush his interests finally lured him away from Australia. In 1898 he emigrated with his entire family to England, where from the 'old world' he published reminiscences and memoirs filled with honest and vibrant images of the Australian outback.

Venus was one of three statues donated to the City of Adelaide by William Austin Horn and is a visible memento of his philanthropic spirit. The statue's unveiling caused a sensation and attracted inevitable moral indignation but Horn resisted all attempts to confine it to a gallery, preferring that it be located outdoors to educate, refine and delight passers-by.

Antonio Canova (1757–1822) was a Florentine sculptor who popularised the neo-classical style. His most famous work was a nude Napoleon but his more demure pieces were adapted from ancient Greek studies. Venus, startled as she steps from her bath, was a common theme in Classical Greece. The statue that graces the city of Adelaide is a copy of the work carved by Canova for Thomas Hope in the 19th century, and Horn may well have visited the copyists, probably the brothers Pugi whose mark appears on the base, in Florence.

Mayor Bullock gave the opening address but avoided any impropriety by allowing his wife to unveil the naked goddess to the large crowd. He obviously had little faith in his fellow citizens and enjoined his audience to protect the statue while reminding them that it had been deliberately placed near the guard station of Government House. However the guards offered little protection and vandals have periodically left their mark on the graceful goddess, including black hand prints on her curves.

The statue has been relocated twice. During the upgrading of the North Terrace gardens in 1930 it was removed from its original site near the corner of King William Street and North Terrace and placed beside the museum and moved again in the 1960s to make way for the Bonython fountain.

References

Advertiser, 5 September 1892, p 4; 20 October 1965, p 2

Adelaide City Council Archives, File No F64R 1930

Licht, F *Canova*, New York, 1983

Nairn, B *Australian Dictionary of Biography*, Melbourne
    University Press, 1983, p 367

Scales, M *John Walker's Village*, Rigby, Adelaide, 1974, p 113

H E R C U L E S

Pennington Gardens, adjacent to Adelaide Oval

Bronze statue on a short pedestal. The heavily muscled figure
is slumped with his left arm over his heavy club and lion
skin cloak. Unveiled 4 October 1892.

The bronze figure of Hercules, another gift of William Austin
Horn, was donated at the same time as the Venus, and was
presumably acquired on the same travels through Europe. It is
a copy of the Farnese Hercules which was excavated in Naples
and found to be signed by the Athenian sculptor Glykon, a
copyist who worked in Roman times. The Hercules was a copy
of a famous statue made in the 4th century BC by Lyssipus,
a Greek sculptor, who was so frequently imitated he created a
new canon of proportions. This style is clearly visible in the
exaggerated, hard muscles of Hercules and a head looking too
small for the body. Lyssipus worked during the end of the
Classical period and into the Hellenistic period, when themes
became more grandiose and complicated.

Classical Greek sculpture was determinedly stylised to

represent perfection, but it also delighted in catching a moment of action or a mood. Here we see Hercules (or Heracles in true Greek nomenclature) tired by his labours and still haunted by his crimes, with brows set in determination. The off-centre balance and the complicated twists of the torso emphasise the tension in the figure.

That Horn chose Hercules and Venus probably gives an insight into his character, although on a more basic level he simply intended to bring some refinement to both the streets and citizens of Adelaide.

ACC Pictorial Collection

Hercules was sited originally in Victoria Square, surrounded by a garden and railings. The statue was unveiled by Mayor Bullock, who did not have any compunction about pulling off the drapes on this occasion. Horn gave a lighthearted address, but as a major shareholder at Broken Hill he took the opportunity to have a dig at striking miners involved in a violent dispute lasting 18 weeks.

References

Onians, J *Art and Thought in The Hellenistic Age*,
    Thames & Hudson, London, 1979
Register, 5 October 1892, p 6

R O B E R T
B U R N S

**Prince Henry Gardens in front of the State Library,
North Terrace**

Near life-size statue in frock coat with ruffles and riding boots standing on a pedestal. gesturing with his left arm as he stares into the distance. The carved facing on the plinth identifies the subject and a dedicatory plaque at the base recalls the beneficence of the South Australian Caledonian Society and its Chief, the Honourable John Darling MLC. Unveiled 5 May 1894.

A statue to the memory of Robert Burns bears the honour of being the first statue carved in Adelaide. Burns seems an unlikely recipient of such an honour in a country so far removed from his heather-carpeted hills, but Scottish pomp and pageantry were in high fashion throughout the Empire, and South Australia had no shortage of the descendants of dispossessed crofters and opportunist lowlanders. At a Caledonian concert in the Town Hall to mark Burns's birthday in 1893 it was noted that Ballarat had just erected a statue to the bard, and the good Scots citizens of Adelaide hastened to follow. Sir Thomas Elder and Robert Barr-Smith gave the initial donations and John Darling (1831–1905) the Chief of the Caledonian Society gave his blessing.

The statue committee, insisting that the work be entirely of colonial manufacture, gave the task to William Maxwell, Adelaide's premier sculptor. This colonial loyalty had the advantage of producing quick results, since it took only 15 months from proposal to finished product. Maxwell was also a Scot. Born in 1840 in Largs, Ayrshire, he had migrated to Australia on medical advice in the 1870s, initially settling in Melbourne before being enticed to Adelaide by Robert Barr-Smith in his role as President of the British Architects' Association. Maxwell, the son of a builder and brought up as a stone cutter, had developed his artistic talents under the direction of JB Phillips who had worked on the Albert Memorial in London. Before his departure to Australia, Maxwell completed a model of Robert Burns which won a silver medal at Kilmarnock, this experience probably helping speed his work on the Adelaide commission.

William Maxwell's patrons were the mercantile and commercial lions of Adelaide, who were busily erecting banks and public buildings. He carved Corinthian capitals, cornerstones, friezes and tracery on numerous buildings, including the Savings Bank of South Australia, Parliament House, the Commercial Bank and the Mitchell Building. The allegorical figure of Industry on the Savings Bank building that once stood in Currie Street was reputed to be his best work but other fine examples can be seen in the friezes and keystone of the Bank of South Australia building, now known as Edmund Wright House, in King William Street.

After a brief return to Scotland, Maxwell purchased the Woodlands estate in Edwardstown which he transformed into a Gothic castle complete with gargoyles. In 1958 it was converted into the Castle Motor Hotel, which in turn was demolished to make way for the Castle Plaza shopping centre. Maxwell died at his home in 1903 after a sudden illness and before he could complete the Stuart memorial. Much of his carving has been lost to development, and few of Adelaide's residents realise their debt to this decorator in stone.

The Burns memorial was unveiled in perfect weather before a large crowd. The invited guests wore a sprig of heather imported from Scotland for the occasion and the *Advertiser* reported that they were regaled with 'scotch' music. John Darling performed the ceremony and gave a long speech describing the career of the poet. Darling was the founder of a grain and milling business and his export success was a boon to the ailing South Australian economy in the 1890s.

The Burns statue was originally located on the corner of Kintore Avenue and North Terrace, but the site was earmarked for the city's war memorial during the redevelopment of the North Terrace gardens. Burns was moved in 1930 and placed beside the entrance to the Art Gallery, to the delight of the Caledonian Society which tendered their fulsome thanks to the council for choosing this prominent site. Unfortunately it was a little too prominent for the Board of Governors of the Gallery who thought the statue disrupted the symmetry of the Gallery's façade and that its positioning would be 'subject to criticism and ridicule by those who are competent to judge'. On the intercession of the Premier, Mr Thomas Playford, the statue was moved again in 1940 to its present site.

References

Adelaide City Council Archives, File No 2617, 1938;
    File No F64R, 1930

Advertiser, 21 July 1903, p 6

Dowie, J 'The Master Carver', *Kalori*, December 1963, p 13

Observer, 12 May 1894, p 14

Pascoe, JJ *Adelaide and Vicinity*, 1901, p 416

Scarlett K *Australian Sculptors*, Thames Nelson, 1980, p 422

QUEEN VICTORIA

The junction of Grote and Wakefield Streets, Victoria Square

Life-size bronze statue of Queen Victoria on a tall and elaborate pedestal emblazoned with the title 'Victoria RI' and depicted by the sculptor as the severe matriarch of the British Empire, heavily robed, crowned by a tiara, securely clutching the royal sceptre and orb and gazing impassively down King William Street. A small inscription at the base records that the statue was presented by the 'Hon Sir Edwin Thomas Smith KCMG MLC 1894'. Unveiled 11 August 1894.

Monarchs become more popular with age and Queen Victoria graced the British throne for longer than any other, her name ultimately describing an epoch. Her stern features are recognisable the world over, and can cause the modern observer to wonder what sparked the legendary enthusiasm and love of her loyal subjects. The good Queen was given pride of place in Adelaide, at the geographical heart of the city. When Queen Victoria's statue was erected, King William

Street ran through the centre of Victoria Square and the intersection of the two roadways was the centre of Colonel Light's city plan.

In the 1890s Adelaide was again in the midst of an economic depression but was proud of its beautiful streets and parks, and it was this statue's donor, Sir Edwin Thomas Smith, who must be credited with much of that beautification. As Mayor during the prosperous 1880s he championed improvement, asphalting the city streets, laying gas lighting, placing deep drainage, damming the Torrens, and planting and beautifying the squares. This fine bronze statue was the *piece de resistance*, yet one cannot help thinking that it should be Sir Edwin standing up there.

Sir Edwin's long and distinguished public career began as Mayor of Norwood in the 1870s and included 20 years in parliament. Norwood was an early beneficiary of his vision when he secured and established the Norwood Oval. He was a member of most of the service and sporting associations in Adelaide and gained his knighthood for organising the Jubilee Exhibition in 1888 when government timidity threatened its success. If that were insufficient reason for his popularity then his Kent Town brewery provided the colony with all the cheer it needed. The brewery which he established soon after his arrival from Scotland in 1853 was so successful that he was able to retire in 1888. Smith's endowments and public works are largely unrecognised but it is fitting that the name of this avid fan of the noble recreations adorns Adelaide Oval's stately Victorian stand.

The statue was chosen by Sir Edwin Smith when he visited England in 1893 and offered to the City Council on his return. It was cast in England at the Thames and Dutton foundry from a model by Charles Bell Birch. Thames and Dutton had already cast nine other statues of the solemn Queen, including one for Sydney, so this foundry was probably the natural choice. Birch (1832–1893) specialised in portraiture busts and medallions and flourished in the 1880s, sculpting gentry and politicians, including Benjamin Disraeli. He studied at the Berlin and Royal Academy schools and spent ten years as a pupil and assistant of Henry Foley. There is little imagination in the pose and visage of the monarch but, to be fair, there was little latitude for innovation. Queen Victoria had fostered an image and her adoring subjects would not have recognised a smiling monarch.

The unveiling was scheduled for a Saturday and, forever the populist and sporting enthusiast, Sir Edwin chose 4 pm to allow the football and race patrons to attend after their usual activities. Unfortunately, the large ceremonial array of police and firemen meant that most of the crowd could not hear the speeches. The Governor, Lord Kintore, gave a simple address, remarking that Adelaide had the perfect climate for statues.

The good Queen has remained an unsmiling hazard to traffic ever since and has resisted, with a becoming stubbornness, all efforts to move her. She stands there imperious and impervious, as a symbol of colonial loyalty.

References

Burgess, H *Cyclopedia of South Australia*, 1907, p 443

Register, 11 August 1894, p 4; 13 August 1894, p 5

Serle, G *Australian Dictionary of Biography*, vol 6, 1976, p 147

EGYPTIAN COLUMN

South Australian Museum courtyard, North Terrace

Stone column with capital, standing at the central point of
the courtyard. Engraved with reliefs and hieroglyphs.
Unveiled 7 July 1899.

One of the oldest architectural monuments in Australia, the
Egyptian column forms the apex of the traffic island in the
South Australian Museum's courtyard. It once stood on the
ancient banks of the River Nile, first in the vestibule of the
temple of the god Heru-shefit at Sutenhenen and later at
Heracleopolis, closer to the Nile Delta. Heru-shefit (or
Heryshaf) is a little-known ram-headed god, prominent in
middle Egypt, whose temple was built by the great Pharaoh
Rameses the Second around 1200 BC. Semi-obliterated
inscriptions which can just be detected on the north-western
face of the column shaft suggest that the column may have
been used in an even earlier structure.

The column was a gift from the Egyptian Exploration
Fund but the motivation for this stroke of good fortune is

obscure. The honorary secretary of the Fund, Miss Amelia B Edwards, made the offer in a letter in 1892. At this time the Museum was an overcrowded building which did not have room for an Egyptian display and no connection with the Fund is known. The column was in two fragments and lacked a capital, but a plaster cast from an identical column in the British Museum was acquired. The cost of reproducing the capital was defrayed by George Brookman (1850–1927), another of Adelaide's mining philanthropists.

Brookman was a financier and stock broker who formed a syndicate to mine gold in the new field at Kalgoorlie in 1893. The syndicate was late on the scene and pegged a large claim in an unwanted area which was thereafter sardonically known as 'Brookman's sheep run': it proved to be the richest lode in Western Australia, returning a steady flow of gold to the South Australian economy. Brookman continued the tradition of the Victorian age by becoming a conservative politician interested in natural history and capitalism. He was on the Board of Governors of the Art Gallery and the Museum and received a knighthood in 1920.

The capital was carved by local masons from a seven ton granite block quarried at Swanport. It is modelled on a lotus flower, and the square cushion on top was an Egyptian architectural trick to raise the cross beams from the capital, giving the architrave an appearance of floating above the columns. Brookman had earned the right to lower the capital onto the erected column before the large crowd. He was followed by the president of the Board of Governors, the erudite and energetic Sir Samuel Way, who gave a vote of thanks and used the occasion to enlighten his audience about Egyptian history.

*Detail of Rameses offering gifts
to god Heru Shefit*

Ancient Egyptian columns are rare on this side of the world, but perhaps the ambience of the Museum courtyard lessens the surprise. On the south-western side the hieroglyphs praise the Pharaoh Rameses, proclaiming him 'King of the South and North, son of the sun, beloved of Aten, living forever'. Three thousand years later an audience of lunchers and schoolchildren can still see Rameses offering gifts to the god Heru-shefit.

References

Advertiser, 8 July 1899, p 6

Australian, 9 January 1982, Weekend Magazine, p 8

Hart, G *A Dictionary of Egyptian Gods and Goddesses*, Routledge, London, 1986

Nairn, B (ed) *Australian Dictionary of Biography*, vol 7, 1979, p 479

Pascoe, JJ *Adelaide and Vicinity*, 1901, p 398

Records of SA Museum – correspondence from museum's education office

Register, 8 July 1899, p 6

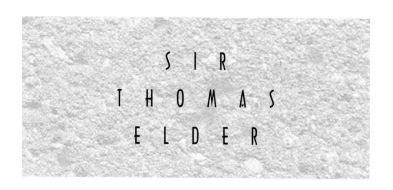

SIR THOMAS ELDER

University of Adelaide, in front of the Elder
Conservatorium, North Terrace

Larger than life-size bronze statue standing on tall stone
pedestal bearing bronze reliefs on three sides with representations of Elder's achievements and a decorative bronze shield
on the fourth side. Unveiled 29 July 1903.

The Elder name is a familiar one in Adelaide, where Sir
Thomas Elder was a generous benefactor. Undoubtedly one
of Adelaide's wealthiest and most powerful individuals, he
gave the city a thriving pastoral company, a park, a rotunda,
a concert hall and a conservatorium, and on his death in
1897 he left most of his estate to public institutions and charities. The largest single recipient of his largesse which
amounted to £103 000, was the University of Adelaide, and he
also supported the Art Gallery, the Botanic Gardens and the
Zoological Gardens, to which he gave another rotunda and
an elephant! Little wonder that the people of Adelaide sought
to ensure his memory with a bronze statue. It is situated,

appropriately, in the grounds of the university he helped to found.

Sir Thomas Elder left few private records or letters to give an insight into his life and character. He was born in Kirkcaldy, Scotland, in 1841 and followed his brother to Adelaide in 1854, eventually taking over the partnership in a burgeoning pastoral company. He then combined with his brother-in-law Robert Barr-Smith to form a commercial empire. Fortune favoured Elder, Smith and Co. when it capitalised the copper mining ventures of Walter Watson Hughes at Wallaroo and later Moonta. The massive returns from these mines enabled the company to expand its pastoral holdings throughout the state, especially in the north, and financed the unique fencing and well-digging programs which helped establish a viable grazing empire amongst the ruins of drought stricken cereal farms.

The young Thomas Elder certainly did not follow the dour Scottish mercantile stereotype – he was adventurous and travelled widely in North Africa, Palestine and Spain. He expounded on the virtues of travel and put his convictions and experience to practical use when, although not the first to realise the potential of camels in the dry inland, he succeeded in establishing a camel-breeding stud on his station at Beltana which supplied explorers, telegraph builders and the communities of central Australia until the turn of the century.

In later life he fulfilled his public duties as a member of the Legislative Council but otherwise took little part in directing public affairs. He dabbled in horse breeding and was commodore of the Glenelg Yacht club but remained a reclusive bachelor who generally avoided public life, dividing

The Muses frieze

his time between his homes 'Birksgate' at Glen Osmond and 'The Pinnacles' at Mount Lofty. He was knighted in 1878 and received the much rarer distinction of GCMG in 1887.

Sir Samuel Way led the rush to provide a memorial and chaired the statue committee from 1898. A bronze memorial was decreed suitable and Way rejected as 'impudent' approaches from James White, a Sydney sculptor, in favour of some 'competent' English sculptor. Through the Agent-General in London the final choice devolved upon Alfred Drury. The statue and panels were to be cast and delivered to Adelaide for a fee of £900. Drury subsequently attempted to raise his fee and was held to his original quote by the pugnacious Way, but there was then a price to be paid in interminable delays. The pedestal was finally in place by October 1902 but the worthy subscribers still had plenty of time to

New Generation given over to the University frieze

debate which way Sir Thomas should face while they waited for the arrival of the statue. By March 1903 Way was reduced in his correspondence with London to threats of no future commissions, but the colonial memorial now had to wait in line behind the coronation statues of King Edward VII.

The unveiling in July 1903 was a gala occasion led by the Governor, Sir George Ruthven Le Hunte, but the solemnity was disturbed by a procession of students blowing tin whistles and catcalling from the university windows. The practical jokers, who were simply trying to emulate their Oxford and Cambridge counterparts, earned the ire of all present, as well as general condemnation in the local press.

Sir Thomas was placed facing away from the university he had so generously endowed. He stands rather pompously with one hand clasping his lapel, a position which has

Camel Train frieze decorating Sir Thomas Elder pedestal

prompted other student pranksters to add painted swords to his apparel. The 12 feet (3.7 m) high pedestal of Aberdeen granite was the gift of an anonymous donor and cost £266. The panels are more interesting than the statue. On the western panel a female figure holds a model of the Mitchell Building and is flanked by a mother with baby, and the figure of Medicine. This is meant to symbolise the giving of today's children to the care of the university, producing the esteemed professionals of the future. The eastern panel represents the muses with Painting, Music, and Literature in the foreground and Sculpture peeping from behind. A winding camel train on the northern panel, an appropriate reminder of Elder's practical assistance in the exploration of the colony, is probably the least successful.

While many of Adelaide's statues represent a wealthy elite whose achievements seem less memorable with passing years, Sir Thomas Elder's generosity has left its mark on our folk memory, and while the active heart of the university has moved away from the common where his monument stands, its quieter repose would probably have suited this reclusive man.

References

Burgess, H *Cyclopedia of South Australia*, 1907, p 260

Gosse, F *Sir Thomas Elder*, paper presented to the Royal Geographical Society of Australasia, SA Branch, 29 September 1962

'SJ Way on the Elder Statue', *South Australiana*, vol 13 no 2, 1974, p 105

Advertiser, 30 July 1903, p 6

Register, 30 July 1903, p 8

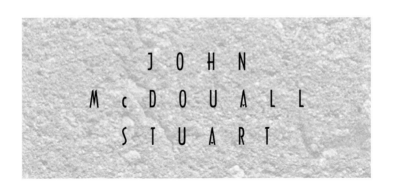

JOHN McDOUALL STUART

North-eastern corner of Victoria Square

Life-size statue in Carrara marble dressed in bush costume, draped with a Union Jack over the left shoulder, standing in a rigid photographic pose on an elaborate stepped plinth with an ill-drawn map of Australia facing. Also facing is a plaque bearing the inscription 'John McDouall Stuart Explorer Adelaide to Indian Ocean'. Stuart is grasping a copy of his journal in his right hand, and his helmet, saddle and sextant are scattered about his feet. Unveiled 4 June 1904.

Manning Clark described John McDouall Stuart as an 'extravagant exaggerator whose face lit up when he got within 500 miles of a hotel'. However, he was a tough determined man and it was not merely thirst that impelled him to complete the first successful return journey through the centre of Australia in 1862. Between 1858 and 1862 he led six expeditions to the arid north of South Australia, initially for pastoralists and then for the government.

Stuart had come to the colony of South Australia in

1838 as a surveyor but he became convinced that fame and fortune were to be found on the frontier. The 1850s and 1860s were the great eras of exploration and the feats and discoveries of these adventurers were greeted with similar enthusiasm to those of the astronauts 100 years later. From 1861 this excitement was enlivened by a race between South Australia and Victoria to the northern coast of Australia. Stuart's triumphant return coincided with the solemn procession of the mortal remains of Burke and Wills through Adelaide in January 1863. On 21 January crowds lined the streets to see the scarecrow Stuart, and to pull his carriage down North Terrace. But the financial rewards were less generous for Stuart and the journeys had exacted a heavy toll. He returned to England a tired and prematurely aged man, and doubtless the ravages of scurvy accelerated the onset of the cerebral haemorrhage which killed him on 5 June 1866.

Despite his shortcomings the people of South Australia remembered Stuart and when in 1895 on the anniversary of his journey, a group of friends from the Survey Department, including some survivors of the expedition, gathered to drink a toast, the spirit of the moment sparked a movement to erect a permanent monument. A committee established under the leadership of one of the survivors, WP Auld, initiated a 'shilling fund' and a call for donations raised £182. There the matter rested until it was taken up by the Caledonian Society which succeeded in raising a further £570 and obtaining a government grant for a similar amount. The Society had already organised the erection of a statue to Robert Burns and they chose the same local sculptor, William Maxwell, to do this work. Maxwell's model survives in the reading room of the Mortlock Library of South Australiana,

but he died before he could carve the Carrara marble he had insisted upon importing after a search for suitable local stone had failed to satisfy him.

Another Scottish sculptor living in Sydney, James White, was chosen to finish the work using Maxwell's design. At the turn of the century White was one of the few sculptors in Australia working in bronze, and by 1904 he had completed statues in Perth, Sydney and Bendigo and had worked for the prominent South Australian, Sir Edwin Thomas Smith. White's largest works including the Queen Victoria Memorial in Melbourne and the stiff and uninspired Boer War Memorial in Bendigo, were executed later.

The unveiling proved to be a cantankerous, curmudgeonly affair. The original committee was particularly annoyed that the survivors of the historic trip were not given a prominent role and the affair degenerated into a public slanging match culminating in a boycott by the four survivors. Auld tried to enlist the support of the Royal Geographical Society and the Adelaide City Council to circumvent the Caledonian Society's arrangements and made much of the fact that the Governor had declined the honour of unveiling. When the proceedings continued regardless, the vitriolic exchange continued in the local papers with Auld petitioning the council to remove the plaque at the base of the statue which proclaimed the involvement of the Caledonian Society.

Such was the regard for the hard-drinking Stuart that the unveiling by the president of the Society drew a large crowd, and an even larger one filed past on the next day, a Sunday. Much was made of the fact that his epic journey had blazed a trail for the overland telegraph, which left the colonies in his eternal debt. Stuart would have been happier with more earthly payments, but his petitions for reward had been largely ignored by the government. Cheated by fortune, his fame is celebrated by the highway bearing his name heading north across the arid continent.

References

Advertiser, 31 May 1904, p 6; 3 June 1904, p 6; 4 June 1904, p 6; 6 June 1904, p 7

Burgess, H *Cyclopedia of South Australia*, 1907, p 9

Nairn, B (ed) *Australian Dictionary of Biography*, vol 6, 1976, p 214

Scarlett, K *Australian Sculptors*, Thomas Nelson, Melbourne, 1980, p 687

Royal Geographical Society of Australasia, SA Branch, Proceedings, vol 7, 1903/04

SOUTH AFRICAN WAR MEMORIAL

**North-eastern corner of the intersection
King William Street and North Terrace**

Life-size bronze statue of a mounted Australian Bushman sharply reigning his horse on the summit of a rocky outcrop resembling a typical South African 'kopje'. Standing on a granite pedestal, with bronze plaques on four sides, commemorating the South Australians who died in the war. Unveiled 6 June 1904.

The South African War Memorial towers over the passing traffic on a majestic site. This was Adelaide's first war memorial and it was given pride of place in front of Government House, looking toward Parliament House. The animation and tension of the tightly reigned horse makes it the most eye-catching statue in Adelaide.

The patriotic response to the British setbacks in South Africa was fuelled by Adelaide's newspapers calling for volunteers and donations. South Australia sent nine contingents, including 1534 officers and men and 1430 horses.

A memorial committee, chaired by the philanthropist George Brookman, was formed immediately at the end of the war. Over £2500 was subscribed by the public with an alacrity which later statue committees must have envied.

All of Adelaide's early bronze statues were carved and cast in England. Negotiations and supervision of the work were always difficult and the memorial committee formed an ad hoc subcommittee of members holidaying in London, assisted by the Agent-General. The committee's original intention was to obtain a secondhand model of 'horse and rider' which with only slight alterations would be suitable. Captain Adrian Jones was recommended by the Agent-General as 'a man exceedingly good for horses' who would do the work 'far cheaper than anyone else'. Jones showed the committee a model made for a competition in South Africa and offered them a replica at the bargain price of £2000, but only if the original were accepted in South Africa. He also produced a lively sketch of a single rider reaching a summit and said that if the committee chose this work immediately he would endeavour to complete it in bronze, standing 11 feet (3.4 m) high, for the fee of £1600. This, he emphasised, was virtually cost price but it would enable him to keep his studio staff employed while awaiting the larger South African commission. Sensing a bargain and pleased with the sketch the committee looked no further. Jones was given just one week to present a model and, by his own account, stunned the colonial experts with the speed of the work.

Captain Jones was a trained veterinarian and a career officer in the army with an interest in art. He saw active service in India, Abyssinia and Egypt but had sufficient means to open and maintain a studio in London, so keeping

A huge crowd at the unveiling of the South African War Memorial on 6 June 1906
SSL: MB8831

company with artists. Much of his 20-year army career seems to have been spent sketching, with Jones having a particular affinity for animals. As a member of the horse and hunting set, his talents were soon used to immortalise race horses and hounds. Jones's first foray into the Royal Academy in 1892 had led to controversy and mutual disdain, when the art luminaries accused him of using 'ghost' sculptors to produce his work. Despite gentlemanly outrage and demands for satisfaction this scandal was never settled. Jones's supporters were mainly from amongst the mounted gentry, and when the committee from Adelaide arrived, Jones had just received Royal patronage from the Prince of Wales.

Jones described his design as vigorous, intended to appeal to the 'sturdy Australian people'. The plaster model was presented to his home town, Ludlow, in Shropshire. The South Australian Boer war veterans believed the mounted figure to be modelled on Quartermaster Sergeant George Goodall who, as part of the Australian Corps at the coronation of Edward VII, had been delegated to advise Jones on uniform details. Goodall may well have been persuaded to model for the head of the trooper but Jones's memoirs do not mention any sittings.

Although Jones devoted most of his career to war memorials his martial monuments are counterbalanced by his most famous work, the Peace Quadriga on Constitution Hill, London, which was completed in 1912. His talents also grace Adelaide's streets in the shape of Captain Sturt's memorial, a statue located in the centre of Adelaide.

The 12 feet high pedestal of the Boer War Memorial was quarried from Murray Bridge granite. A competition was held and the winning design, which was subject to minor alterations by the artist, was selected from 12 submissions. The bronze plaques were also crafted locally from gun plates.

The memorial was unveiled on 6 June 1904, then a public holiday for the birthday of the Prince of Wales. Fittingly, it was also the third anniversary of the battle of Graspan, where South Australian combatants had distinguished themselves by capturing a Boer convoy. The day was dull but dry and the large crowd included a complete parade of the Boer war contingents. An enclosure was provided for the widows and mothers of the fallen. The short ceremony included speeches from George Brookman, Governor Le Hunte and the contingents' military commander, whose bright scarlet uniform with white plumed hat drew a cry of 'cock-a-doodle-do' from a comic in the crowd.

Governor Le Hunte (1852–1925) released the Union Jack and canvas drapes to reveal the statue which now stood at the entrance to his residence. Le Hunte, a barrister, had chosen to follow a diplomatic career. His apprenticeship was served in the West Indies and the Pacific, where he was Lieutenant-Governor of British New Guinea before his appointment as the King's representative in South Australia from 1 July 1903 to 31 December 1908.

The Boer war brought few traumas to Adelaide and its dramatic, beautiful memorial was designed to capture and convey the excitement of action. Today, with the last of the veterans long dead, only this straining mounted scout peering intently at the city bustle reminds us of the colonial endeavour which cemented imperial ties. Those same imperial ties were soon to embroil the population of Adelaide in a far greater conflagration which was to change the mood of subsequent war memorials.

References

Advertiser, 1 July 1903, p 6; 19 October 1967, p 4

Mortlock Library of South Australiana, Research Note 213

Jones, A *Memoirs of Soldier Artist*, London, Stanley Paul and Co., 1933

Murray, PL *Records of Australian Contingents to the War in South Africa*, National Memorial Fund, Minute Book, 1911, Mortlock Library of South Australiana, V498

Observer, 11 June 1904, p 40

RK Thomas Album, Mortlock Library of South Australiana, V1466

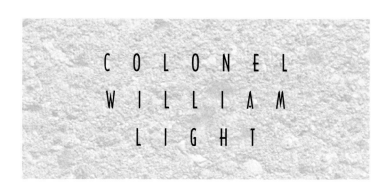

COLONEL WILLIAM LIGHT

'Light's Vision', Montefiore Hill lookout, Pennington Terrace

Life-size bronze, dressed in full military regalia, with one hand holding a map and the other pointing towards the centre of the city he planned, raised on a granite pedestal and forming the centrepiece of a balustraded garden lookout. An inscription on the front of the pedestal states: 'Colonel William Light first surveyor general, fixed the site and laid out the city of Adelaide in 1836. Erected by citizens 1906.' On the back of the pedestal is a wreath added by the first Australian town planning conference held in Adelaide in 1917, and reproduced below is an extract from Light's Journal where he thanks his enemies for giving him the sole responsibility of choosing the site of Adelaide. Unveiled 27 November 1906.

The citizens of Adelaide have long been proud of their planned city, happily giving credit to the colony's first surveyor, Colonel William Light. Light had an interesting mixture of skill, recklessness, flair and mystery which made

him genuinely popular with his contemporaries and a legendary figure to their descendants. The legend was so strong that it was 80 years before the city fathers realised how few historical facts relating to Light were known. It was the approaching centenary of the city that prompted a rush to gather information regarding his birth and career. The researchers took 30 years to produce a clear picture from the myths. His birth date was not discovered until 1966, in the baptismal records of a Roman Catholic mission in Malaya. William Light was born on 27 April 1786 at Kuala Kedah in Malaya, the illegitimate son of Captain Francis Light. His mother is unknown, possibly Portuguese or Eurasian, and the frequently claimed link with Malayan royalty is fanciful. He was raised in Suffolk by family friends. In 1799 he joined the navy, but the ebb and flow of the Napoleonic wars led him to an army career and distinguished service in the Peninsular campaign.

By the end of the war Colonel Light was described as a distinguished artist, painter, soldier and sailor but opportunities were few, and he was to spend most of his time cruising the Mediterranean, sketching and painting. However, he had influential friends who proposed him as governor of the new colony of South Australia, where his experience of the Mediterranean was held to be a great asset. He was offered instead the position of surveyor-general and held in sufficient esteem to be given the sole responsibility of choosing the site for the new capital, a task made difficult by the number of powerful officials and colonists who dogged his heels and tried to influence his decision.

After completing his blueprint for the city, a disappointed Light resigned in June 1838. The following year he

The unveiling of Colonel Light in Victoria Square, 27 November 1906
ACC Pictorial Collection

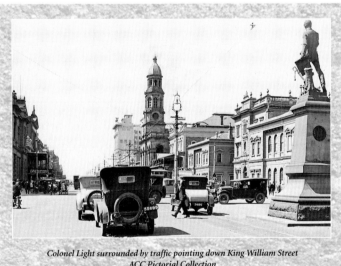

Colonel Light surrounded by traffic pointing down King William Street
ACC Pictorial Collection

died of tuberculosis, leaving a lasting impression of a man badly treated by authority and driven to an early grave. However, Light had plenty of friends in the new city of Adelaide, and though his death came only three years after settlement, there was already a feeling of public gratitude (and perhaps guilt) and a desire to preserve his memory. The decision to bury him in the city square bearing his name was a singular honour, and within one week £250 had been collected towards a memorial. A total of £641 was raised and George Kingston designed an elaborate Gothic cross, carved from sandstone, that was erected in 1843.

By 1892 the original monument, had become so badly weathered that Mayor Bullock called a meeting to form a committee to erect 'a substantial monument' to Colonel Light. Initial enthusiasm was high and subscriptions raised £348, with the City Council pledging £500 and the government £1000. However, South Australia was by that time stumbling into economic depression marked by disastrous bank failures and widespread unemployment. Subsequently, despite frequent deputations, the government reneged on its promised support and the proposed competition to select a design came to nothing, and the committee lapsed.

Twelve years later a meeting of subscribers launched another deputation to lay siege to the State treasury's coffers, this time with success. Their pent-up frustration was immediately released in a flurry of activity: a new committee called for new designs and caused some consternation when it was decided not only to replace the grave monument but also to erect a separate statue.

A theodolyte on a tall column was chosen for the Light Square memorial, and was unveiled first, on 21 June 1905, before a large crowd which included honoured guests who had witnessed Light's funeral 66 years before. Sir Samuel Way gave the address and seized the opportunity to relate Light's adventures and achievements, reinforcing the established legend. It was a gala occasion, made more so by the donation to the South Australian Art Gallery of a self-portrait previously in the possession of the Mayo family.

For the statue, the committee chose a design by the Scottish sculptor Birnie Rhind. Trained by his father and working in Edinburgh, Rhind specialised in architectural work. He had produced the usual array of royal sculptures for Indian cities and his association with Australia had already begun when he provided one for Melbourne. The committee's notes and papers have not been saved, so the inspiration for the design is unknown. Light stands in dress uniform holding a map in his left hand while woodenly pointing with his extended right arm. The statue was completed for £1000 and the pedestal, designed by the local architects Garlick, Sibley and Wooldridge, for £510.

The City Council decided to place the statue in Victoria Square, at the intersection with King William Street and pointing aimlessly down the busy thoroughfare. Victoria Square was the geographical centre of the city and, as the worthy speakers at the unveiling made abundantly clear, the city fathers intended to fill it with noble explorers and dignitaries. The unveiling was virtually a re-enactment of the graveside ceremony. Sir Samuel Way declined the honour of repeating his address but was not above criticising Mayor Bruce for his boring recitation of the committee's long tribulations. The statue was officially unveiled by Governor Le Hunte, who noted that little had changed since Light's time as the Crown still ignored the advice of the man on the spot.

Colonel Light's statue, somewhat ironically, was soon to become the centre of a planning dispute with traffic threatening its serenity. The earliest request to remove it as a traffic hazard appears in the council minutes in 1908, and the litany of complaints was to grow louder. Light was soon surrounded by whirring trams and hemmed in by crisscrossing wires, which ran down the length of King William Street. However, it was not until the state's centenary in 1936 that the question of Light's statue was given serious consideration, prompted by the development of a lookout on Montefiore Hill as a celebratory project. The lookout was originally intended to honour the state's pioneers but the President of the Pioneer Association, Sir Henry Newland suggested renaming it 'Light's Vision' and shifting the statue on the centenary of Light's death. Again ironically, it took many changes of plan before Light, the doyen of city planners, was moved in 1938. The Colonel now stands majestically overlooking his city, proudly claiming credit for all before him.

References

Adelaide City Council Archives, File No 153C

Colonel William Light-Founder of Adelaide, Adelaide City Year Book 1961, author unattributed but largely written by Mr DF Elder

Rees, JS 'Memorials to the Founder of Adelaide', Mortlock Library of South Australiana, Pamphlet 1950

Register, 28 November 1906, p 6; 22 June 1905, p 6; 15 September 1933, p 5

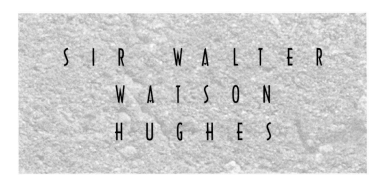

SIR WALTER WATSON HUGHES

University of Adelaide grounds, in front of the entrance to the Mitchell Building

Bronze statue seated on a rectangular granite pedestal, identified on a plaque facing North Terrace as 'Sir Walter Watson Hughes one of the Founders of, and the first donor to this University'. Unveiled 28 November 1906.

Sir Walter Watson Hughes spent just 27 years in Adelaide but succeeded in amassing a fortune and becoming the unintentional 'father' of the university. From accounts given by his contemporaries he was a colourful character. Born in Fifeshire, Scotland, on 22 August 1803, he chose a roving life, initially with the Arctic whalers and then plying the opium trade between India and China. He came to Adelaide in 1840, aboard his own ship the *Hero* and apparently abandoned the sea to become a pastoralist. With South Australia on the brink of financial collapse his initial ventures failed until, in partnership with Captain John Duncan, he acquired properties at Watervale and Wallaroo.

Mineral wealth was one of the great hopes of many of the early colonists and Hughes was the most fortunate of all. When he detected signs of copper on the beach at Wallaroo he instructed his employees to be alert and was rewarded with the discovery of some of the largest copper mines in Australia. His own fortune, as well as the economic foundation of South Australia, were now secured.

Having made good, Hughes chose to return to England for a prolonged sojourn from 1864 to 1870 and then permanently in 1873. He spurned his native Scotland for the milder climate of Surrey, where he died in 1887. It was during his brief return to Adelaide that he donated the princely sum of £20 000 for the foundation of a religious college. However when the Reverend James Jefferies suggested that the money would be better used to found a university, the idea was greeted with enthusiasm by many in the community. The University Association was duly formed with a pessimistic Hughes as president and when he left Adelaide in 1873 he predicted that the venture would be a 'dead failure'. Hughes estimated that between £80 000 and £100 000 would be required. His commercial judgement proved correct, and only the beneficence of Sir Thomas Elder ensured the University of Adelaide's success.

Hughes may have been the first donor, but the generous and ongoing support of Sir Thomas Elder earned Elder the honour of first public recognition by the university. It was the unveiling of Elder's statue in 1903 that prompted Hughes's nephews, John and Walter Duncan, to announce their undertaking to raise a similar bronze memorial to their uncle. The commission was given to Francis Williamson (1833–1920), an English sculptor who was raised and trained in London. The pedestal was also designed by the sculptor and its construction by Mr Laycock of Waymouth Street was supervised by George K Soward, a local architect. Williamson specialised in portrait sculpture and had exhibited at the Royal Academy from as early as 1853. In 1870 he was commissioned by Queen Victoria to execute the memorial to Princess Charlotte and her husband Leopold and thereafter had remained in royal favour. At the Crystal Palace Exhibition in 1851 he exhibited no less than 29 royal busts and statues. His Jubilee bust of Queen Victoria in 1887 was duplicated and despatched all over the world, indelibly setting her stern features throughout the Empire.

The statue was unveiled by Mrs Walter H Duncan whose husband had recently died. The university's luminaries were present and, in accepting the statue from John Duncan, the Chancellor, Sir Samuel Way gave one of his customary lengthy speeches. Sizing up his audience, he took the opportunity to extol the virtues of the university and its achievements in extending the frontiers of knowledge, and to emphasise the need for more professorships, more laboratories and more benefactors.

References

Johnson, J *Dictionary of British Artists*, Antique Collectors Club, 1976

Register, 5 January 1887, p 5; 28 November 1906, p 9

Serle, G *Australian Dictionary of Biography*, Angus & Robertson, 1949, p 461

The Times, 13 March 1920, p 18

Waters, GM *Dictionary of British Artists*, Eastbourne, 1975

ANGAS MEMORIAL

Angas Gardens, near intersection of War Memorial Drive
and King William Road

Marble shrine comprised of a canopy supported by four columns over a memorial pedestal with embossed bronze reliefs on each side depicting achievements of the Angas family, including the transporting of German emigrants, the foundation of South Australia and the annexation of New Zealand. Also relief busts of George Fife Angas, described as 'Patriot, Politician and Philanthropist', and John Howard Angas, described as 'Pioneer Pastoralist and Philanthropist'. Atop the pedestal is an ornate Elizabethan ship. A life size bronze woman with flowing robes and feathered wings ascends the steps of the shrine. No official unveiling.

The Angas name is indelibly linked to the foundation of South Australia. George Fife Angas (1789–1879) began the family connection with the new colony during its planning stages and his nervous energy, coupled with his merchant and banking expertise, helped to establish the commercial viability of the venture. However, it was his hard working son, John Howard Angas (1823–1904) who rescued the financial fortunes of the family and established a dynasty. The pastoral and political success of the Angases gilded by the largesse of their philanthropy, ensured their place in the memory of the community.

The Angas memorial is the most whimsical of Adelaide's standing monuments. It was a gift of the Angas family and is a fanciful display of filial piety in the semblance of a shrine. A public memorial was first mooted after the death of John Angas in 1904 and a site was informally granted in Victoria Square. However that particular site was formally granted to the Sturt statue committee in 1907 and when, in 1909, the Adelaide City Council proposed to allow the Angas family to proceed with their memorial, an outcry erupted. Not all South Australians saw George Angas as a benefactor, and when the Trades and Labour Council weighed into the fray, decrying the public aggrandizement of Angas and complaining that he had been no friend to the worker, to spare further embarrassing argument about the merits of the Angases, the family withdrew their claim to the site.

It was Lilian Gertrude Angas, John's daughter, who provided the final impetus to establishing a fitting memorial to her forebears. Although Lilian had spent only the first 15 years of her life in South Australia she continued the philanthropic traditions of the family in England, supporting and working for a wide range of underprivileged and first world war related charities. She entrusted the supervision of the erection of the memorial to her brother Charles, who controlled the family's affairs.

The memorial is obviously intended as a testament of

achievement and reflects pride in long-held family traditions, such as the 'saving of New Zealand', although George's
role was brief and of marginal importance. The choice of an
Elizabethan ship is obscure, and the angel ostensibly deliv-
ering 'fortune' looks incongruous.

Charles delegated the local architect George K Soward
to oversee the project and was intermittently exasperated by
the whole business. He complained bitterly that the federal
government planned to charge import duty of £440 on the
statue and wrote hurt letters to the City Council when they
refused to fence the finished memorial, regretting that they

did not find it worthy of protection. The delay in its completion would have exasperated anyone. The foundation was laid in April 1913, followed by the canopy, carved in Italy, a year later, and finally by the works of sculpture. It was completed in 1915 at a total cost of over £4000 and perhaps Charles's frustration explains the absence of an official unveiling ceremony.

The memorial was originally sited in the Prince Henry Gardens between Kintore Avenue and King William Street but the 1930 widening of North Terrace and the redevelopment of the gardens resulted in its removal. The council's redevelopment committee suggested the Angas Gardens beside the Torrens as a new site and the memorial was successfully shifted by the local stone masons Ciprano and Co., at a cost of £365.

The sculptor William Robert Colton (1867–1921) designed the canopy and completed the bronzes. Colton had been trained in the Royal Academy's schools and eventually became a professor. He also studied in Paris where he was influenced by Rodin, but his most renowned works are the traditional memorials to King Edward VII at King's Lynn and the South African War Memorial in St James's Park.

References

Adelaide City Council Archives, File No F64R; File No 1629/12

Mortlock Library of South Australiana, PRG 744/3

Pike, D *Australian Dictionary of Biography*, vol 1, 1966, p 15; vol 3, 1969, p 36

Register, 7 May 1915, p 6

Waters, GM *Dictionary of British Artists*, Eastbourne 1975, p 72

The Times, 14 November 1921, p 14

CHARLES
CAMERON
KINGSTON

**South-western corner of the Grote and King William
Streets, Victoria Square**

Life-size statue dressed in the ceremonial garb of a Privy
Councillor complete with sword, frock coat and gaiters and
standing, with right hand raised in an oratorical flourish, on
an elaborately carved pedestal decorated on three sides with
bronze relief panels.

The south-western panel depicts Kingston presiding
over the historic federal convention of 1897, the south-eastern
panel depicts Kingston addressing federal parliament with
fellow federationists, Sir Edmund Barton, Sir John Forrest,
Sir George Turner and Alfred Deakin, and the north-eastern
panel depicts Kingston's father, Sir George Strickland
Kingston.

A bronze coat of arms rests on the cornice of the plinth,
with quartered lions and the motto 'Viribus Scandens' (In
Strength Ascend). The facing inscription reads 'The Right
Honourable Charles Cameron Kingston Patriot and
Statesman'. Unveiled 26 May 1916.

Charles Cameron Kingston was a remarkable politician who strode boldly across public life at the turn of the century, fractiously and recklessly defying the staid burghers of Adelaide. He was both acclaimed as a radical liberal and one of the fathers of the Federation and reviled as a reprobate and stentorian bully. Just the announcement of a movement to erect a statue in his honour was sufficient to trigger angry protests to the newspapers. That such an interesting and enigmatic figure has not suffered a biographer's microscope is equally remarkable.

Kingston was a 'mover and shaker'. Trained to the Bar, he was drawn to politics, first as Attorney-General and then as Premier of South Australia for six years. An early supporter of Federation, he was elected president of the Federal Convention channelling his formidable energy into drafting the Australian Constitution and steering its passage through the British legislature. His career spanned an age of challenge and change and he was a fearless innovator. Amongst his achievements were the introduction of women's suffrage, the extension of progressive taxation and the introduction of industrial arbitration. As Trade Minister in the first federal government he set up the tariff system that established the protectionist policy of the infant nation.

Scandal followed him. He will probably remain the only premier to be arrested for duelling and to be horsewhipped in Victoria Square, both the result of provocative verbal clashes with fellow parliamentarians. Kingston was known for his vicious and spiteful tongue and a tendency to alienate even his friends.

Syphilis cut short his career in 1903, and led to a rapid physical and mental deterioration in his early fifties. He fell under the sway of his difficult and eccentric wife in the last years of his life and his death in 1908 was described as a happy release.

Sir Samuel Way initiated the movement to erect a statue and a small group of Kingston's friends, including Langdon Bonython and William Denny, brought the work to fruition. A large proportion of the funds came from a stranger, a Mr M McNalley, who had never met Kingston, but held him in sufficient esteem to donate £500. Another £187 came from readers of the *Bulletin*, which had always hailed Kingston as a political saviour and promoted his claim to be the first Prime Minister of the Federation.

No records of a formal statue committee have survived, but by 1910 Bonython was requesting a site from the City Council. Alfred Drury was chosen as the sculptor, presumably at the direction of Sir Samuel Way who regarded his work highly, and claimed that the statue of Sir Thomas Elder by Drury was the best in Adelaide. Two of Way's friends and supporters of the project, the Agent-General, Sir John Cockburn, and William Austin Horn, supervised the work in London. Mrs Kingston provided photographs but the identity of the person who chose the garb of a Privy Councillor is a mystery. It seems incongruous that Kingston, who had exerted so much energy battling the notions of 'society' and had refused a knighthood, should be paraded in such frippery.

The sculptor was not entirely successful. Way criticised the panels and thought the portrait of Deakin an utter failure, but all of his pompous ire was reserved for the Superintendent of Public Building, Charles Owen Smyth, who organised the construction of the pedestal by W Laycock.

Bereft of specific guidelines, Owen Smyth had planned to use coloured granite for the base, only to have this criticised as 'piebald' by the opinionated Way, who considered himself an artistic authority. In a messy dispute that ended in parliament Way declared that the sculpture contravened all 'artistic canons', and appeared foolish when example after example was proffered in justification. The level-headed Bonython ended the dispute when he provided a further £50 to add an additional slab of marble between the granite base and the marble column. The fact that Way was mortally ill by this time probably prompted Bonython to intercede.

By the date of the unveiling Way was dead and Denny was fighting in France, which left Bonython to organise the affair. He shrewdly juxtaposed the ceremony with a Premiers' Conference, so there was no shortage of participants. The guest list included all the state Premiers as well as the acting Prime Minister. Sir Edmund Barton, who had worked with Kingston to establish the Federation, made a special trip to honour his colleague. The Governor-General, Sir Ronald Munro-Ferguson, gave a lacklustre address, which is hardly surprising since he had never met Kingston, and unveiled the monument. Munro-Ferguson had a military background and was Governor-General throughout the war years.

Victoria Square was the stage for many dramatic scenes in Charles Cameron Kingston's life and seems a fitting site for his memorial. His friends were keen to honour his memory but they chose a statue that was placid and sedate, capturing little of his fire. The interest in and outrage at his antics have long since died away and his memorial deserves to signify a fuller and richer account of his life. Both South Australia and Australia owe him a debt of memory.

References

Adelaide City Council Archives, File No 6958/10

Advertiser, 28 May 1916, p 9

Campbell, C *Charles Cameron Kingston : Radical Liberal and Democrat*, BA Hons Thesis, University of Adelaide, 1970

Nairn, B *Australian Dictionary of Biography*, vol 9, 1983, p 602

The Unveiling of Charles Cameron Kingston, Record of Proceedings, 1916 Pamphlet, Latrobe, Melbourne

Way, SJ *Letter Books*, Mortlock Library of South Australiana, PRG 630/5

CAPTAIN CHARLES STURT

North-western corner of Victoria Square

Life-size bronze statue dressed in rough open-necked shirt, thick workmanlike pants and a broad brimmed hat, clutching a telescope and map in his left hand, standing with right hand shielding his eyes as he peers rather stiffly at the eastern horizon. Raised on a carved pedestal, which in turn is decorated with four bronze panels. The facing panel reads 'Captain Charles Sturt Explorer born April 28 1793 – died June 16 1869'. The reverse panel names his two principal exploring expeditions, and the eastern and western panels record the members of the two respective parties. Unveiled 21 December 1916.

Captain Charles Sturt provides an interesting study of fame and acclaim fading with time and closer scrutiny. Although Sturt had only spent 12 years in South Australia and his major expedition navigating the Murray River was launched from New South Wales, he was always held in high regard in the junior colony. His contemporaries merited his services highly enough to grant him an annuity on his retirement in 1851, and on his death in 1869 he was already described as 'the father of Australian exploration'. In 1895 his daughter-in-law published a biography which painted a glowing picture of a dashing military hero and an important officer in the colony of New South Wales who had dedicated his life to exploring the unknown wilderness at the cost of his health and wealth.

Around the turn of the century when the citizens of Adelaide began erecting monuments to the founding fathers, Sturt was third in line after John McDouall Stuart and Colonel William Light. Indeed it was at the unveiling of Light's statue in November 1906 that one of the committee members, Robert Kyffin Thomas, proposed Sturt as a deserving recipient of a memorial. The suggestion was clearly popular among the rest of the committee responsible for Light's statue and during their last meeting in December 1906, while still basking in the successful completion of their task, the committee handed the balance of funds collected for Light's memorial to the Mayor of Adelaide to be kept in trust for Captain Sturt. This amounted to only £18 but as a gesture it prompted a torturous ten year process of fund raising, flagging enthusiasm and finally government assistance.

The Sturt memorial movement began enthusiastically enough with a crowded meeting called by Mayor Bruce in the Adelaide Town Hall on 28 February 1907. A large committee was formed and fund raising began but after three years only £374 had been raised from the public. Ironically public enthusiasm for a memorial was revived in response to the suggestion that the memorial to the pioneering family of George Fife Angas appropriate the site originally intended for

Sturt's statue. In April 1907 the Adelaide City Council had granted the north-western portion of Victoria Square to the Captain Sturt memorial yet in 1909 under pressure from the Chief Justice, the eminent Sir Samuel Way, a hastily called rump committee ceded Sturt's right to the position to the Angas family. A wave of support for Sturt ensued, with the local papers eulogising Sturt's achievements and state politicians entering on both sides of the fray. The publicity was just what the statue fund needed, and in addition the state government was prompted to grant a pound for pound subsidy. Yet even with this fillip it took another three years to gather sufficient funds to begin the next stage of selecting a suitable statue. This painfully slow fund-raising demonstrates how little real enthusiasm existed for the so-called 'founding fathers'.

The erection of Sturt's statue seems to have resulted from a sense of duty rather than from overwhelming gratitude. Yet that sense of duty resulted in one of Adelaide's more animated and interesting statues, certainly a contrast to the stiff formality of Stuart's memorial on the opposite corner of Victoria Square. How or why a sculptor was chosen for Adelaide's memorials is often a mystery but with Sturt this is well documented. The committee decided in 1914 to seek a sculptor in London rather than go through the more tedious process of calling for designs. They determined that the statue should be as tall as Light's, which it flanked, and should represent its subject in his 'explorer's garb'.

Only three sculptors, each of whom had successfully completed bronze works on earlier commissions, appear to have been considered: Birnie Rhind, Alfred Drury and Adrian Jones. Drury was highly recommended by a subscriber, probably Sir Samuel Way. A committee was formed in London, including the Agent-General and Sturt's daughter Charlotte, who was pleased to assist with photographs and reminiscences. Charlotte's letters to the committee in Adelaide show she was much taken with Captain Adrian Jones and was delighted when he was chosen; a decision made on the basis of simple sketches rather than models and in which the deciding factor appears to have been cost. Drury offered to do the work for £1200, Rhind for £1000 and Jones for £950. The committee believed it could only afford £900 but accepted Jones's offer.

The clay model Jones produced satisfied Charlotte Sturt but not, from the photographs that were sent, the committee in Adelaide. They were certain the raised hand and the hat would obscure the subject's features, but with Charlotte's support Jones persisted with the design and preserved the animation in this statue that is missing from most of Adelaide's other memorials.

The pedestal and bronze panels were made locally once it was discovered that the cost of using English craftsmen would be far above the committee's means. Even so the pedestal, made from Murray Bridge granite by GE Morgan, cost £620. This left the committee with a £200 deficit that would have been larger had the statue not been shipped free of charge by the P&O Line. The City Council covered the cost of erection but the committee members had to dig into their own pockets once again, probably with a sigh of relief to be finished with the project.

The statue was unveiled by the Governor, Sir Henry Galway, and the Honourable J Lewis, whose father had been a member of Sturt's inland party, gave a detailed account of the brave captain's exploration.

Having been placed on a pedestal it almost seems inevitable that some fall from grace should follow, and a recent revisionist biography of Sturt (E Beale *Sturt. The*

Chipped Idol, Sydney University Press, 1979) attempts to provide a more balanced view. Sadly, many of the stories so faithfully recorded by Sturt's daughter-in-law do not tally with the evidence now presented: far from being a selfless hero, Sturt was a man driven by ambition, restlessly seeking acclaim and prestige. Yet such common frailties seem trivial and the fact remains that Captain Sturt stands high above the crowd because the early colonists and their descendants chose to see him as a symbol of selfless determination and sacrifice.

References

Adelaide City Council Archives, File No 1144/07

Register, 22 December 1916, p 5

Royal Geographical Society of Australasia, SA Branch,
    Manuscript 100c

KING
EDWARD
VII

**Prince Henry Gardens, in front of the Institute Building,
North Terrace**

Slightly larger than life-size statue of King Edward VII dressed
in full coronation regalia and standing on a pedestal 6.4
metres high. On a lower tier stand three female figures
representing Peace, Justice and, with her arms extended and
the fruits of the state crowded at her feet, South Australia.
A simple inscription on the pedestal reads 'Edward VII King
and Emperor 1901–1910'. Unveiled 15 July 1920.

King Edward VII was a popular monarch whose foibles
seemed only to endear him to his subjects. His reputation as
a 'Peacemaker' was enhanced by the conflagration which
followed shortly after his death. His illness was sudden and
brief and his death shocked the Empire. Tributes and eulogies
naturally followed, and it was an opportunity for all far-
flung subjects to affirm their loyalty. The Mayor of Adelaide,
Lewis Cohen, led the way by postponing the mayoral ball and
calling a public meeting to raise a fitting memorial to the late

King. The success of this meeting led to the formation of a memorial committee that was chaired by Cohen and included the leading business figures of Adelaide.

At the second meeting of the committee Sir Samuel Way recommended that Bertram Mackennal, the most famous Australian sculptor of the day, be commissioned to model the work. The committee's confidence was boosted by the excellent response to the appeal, with £4000 raised immediately. Shilling funds run by newspapers and children's penny funds helped, but since the original site proposed for the statue was opposite the Adelaide Club it is reasonable to guess where most of the royal sentiment lay. Cohen personally donated £500 and the Adelaide City Council donated £250, followed later by £100 to add the steps.

Born in 1849, Lewis Cohen emigrated from Liverpool in 1853. He originally settled in Sydney and became involved in the Pacific trade in cotton, copra, trepang and tortoise shell. In 1876 he moved to Adelaide where he opened a branch of the London Loan and Discount Bank. His public-spirited actions earned him a knighthood and a KCMG in 1927. He was an energetic leader who was determined to improve the situation and status of his city. Asphalting Rundle and Hindley Streets undoubtedly earned him the appreciation of his fellow citizens, who also enjoyed the lavish balls he arranged. He held the mayoral office six times up to 1911 and campaigned for Adelaide to be created a lord mayoralty. This was granted in 1919 and he subsequently held that position from 1921 to 1923.

Bertram Mackennal was the first Australian sculptor to be elected to the Royal Academy, albeit as an associate member. He was born in Melbourne in 1863 and was a

contemporary of the Heidelberg painters. Further studies took him to London and Paris before a brief return to Melbourne from 1888 to 1891. The remainder of his working life was spent in London, although he completed many works for his homeland and most Australian galleries have his bronze sculptures. Propagating the likenesses of deceased monarchs initially took up much of his time, with three Queen Victorias, including the one at Ballarat, and at least three other King Edwards. In addition he had the honour of sculpting the recumbent effigies of King Edward and Queen Alexandra for the mausoleum at Frogmore. Not surprisingly, he was knighted for his efforts. Perhaps his most famous work is the sun god Phoebus driving his horses, which crowns Australia House, London.

The long delay between planning the memorial and its fruition is most frequently blamed on the intervention of the first world war but it was also the result of a drawn-out and acrimonious dispute between Mackennal and the committee over the design. The sculptor had originally produced four modelled designs from which the committee chose a standing pose with two supplementary figures representing Peace and Justice. Mackennal had depicted the King as a field marshal: the committee had wanted him to have a more regal appearance but the figure was cast before the committee reminded Mackennal of their wishes. Then with all the pugnacity that Samuel Way could muster, they insisted on the change of apparel. Mackennal complained bitterly that he had never been 'worried by a committee' so severely, and sought the help of King George V to resolve the matter. He finally relented and recast the King but he refused to comply with the committee's request for a third figure to represent

South Australia. Again Way pushed the issue until a com-
promise was reached with a supplementary payment of £250.
The argument had halted the work in 1913, and by the time
it restarted a year later the Great War had intervened.
Mackennal eventually described the figure of South Australia
as the best of the group. The pedestal was also carved by
Mackennal and the complete work cost the kingly sum of
£5750.

Photographs of the unveiling ceremony show a vast
concourse of people crowding the streets and the tops of
buildings. The main attraction was probably the young
martial Prince of Wales, later King Edward VIII, whose visit
to Australia was coincidental but taken advantage of by the
committee which hastily prepared the ceremony. All of
Adelaide society was present, including 500 invited guests
and the Mayor of Melbourne. It is amusing to read that it was
one of the shortest ceremonies on record. All involved must
have been disappointed when the Prince requested that there
be no speeches and literally sprinted up the steps to offer a
brief 'thank you' and unveil his grandfather. His haste is
hardly surprising, since during his short four day stay in
South Australia he had 27 engagements.

King Edward VII's memorial almost abuts the roadway
and so it is difficult to stand back and view Mackennal's
work. The committee's insistence on coronation regalia gives
His Majesty's figure an air of stiff formality and the benign
faces and graceful limbs of the three female figures, all rem-
iniscent of Mackennal's 'Circe', are lost amidst the bustle of
the pavement.

ACC Pictorial Collection

References

Adelaide City Council Archives, File No 753/19

Adelaide City Council Minutes, 1918/19, p 125

'King Edward the Seventh Memorial', Pamphlet, Mortlock
    Library of South Australiana, 1920

Nairn, B *Australian Dictionary of Biography*, vol 8, 1981, p 57

Monument Committee Minute Book, Mortlock Library of South
    Australiana, ADC 496

Scarlett, K *Australian Sculptors*, Thomas Nelson, Melbourne,
    1980, p 403

WOMEN'S WAR MEMORIAL

Pennington Gardens, south-eastern corner of the
intersection of Pennington Terrace and King William Road

Cross of Sacrifice standing 38 feet (11.6 metres) high on its
stepped base at the head of a rectangular hedged garden. The
central aisle of the garden is aligned to point at the façade of
St Peter's Cathedral, which forms an attractive backdrop to
the cross. A plaque on the face of the Cross pays tribute from
the women of South Australia to 'the imperishable memory
of the men who gave their lives in the Great War'. A large
Stone of Remembrance at the opposite end of the garden
reminds all who pass that 'Their name liveth for Evermore'.
Unveiled 25 April 1922.

When gazing from any hill top along the Somme and Ancre
valleys in France, tall crosses and splashes of garden greenery
stand out clearly among farmland fields. Each one represents a carefully tended cemetery, with regimental rows of
gravestones amidst the lawns and rose gardens. The decision at the end of the first world war to leave the dead in their

small hastily dug plots left hundreds of brick-walled English gardens in the towns and fields of northern France. All of the cemeteries are similar and the Cross of Sacrifice, with its Gothic lines and symbolic sword, is a dominant feature.

At the end of the war a small group of Adelaide women were searching for a fitting commemorative shrine for the fallen. At the same time the Commonwealth War Graves Commission came up with the idea to unify the graveyards of France with the symbols of a Sacrificial Cross and a Stone of Remembrance, a notion which caught the imagination of the women in Adelaide, who saw an opportunity to form a tangible link with the distant dead. The Lady Mayoress initiated the scheme on 12 March 1919, by calling a public meeting which set up a committee. The aim was to produce a spontaneous offering from the women of South Australia to their fallen servicemen, and the emotional appeal of that aim is still apparent. Some of the committee members had lost family members, including the secretary, Dorothy Gilbert, who had lost two brothers to unknown graves. They wanted this memorial to be organised entirely by women and were later to boast proudly that only the 'Lion Memorial' at Waterloo could match this claim. They also wanted to inspire as many of the women of South Australia as possible to donate, rather than just a handful of wealthy benefactors. They hoped to raise between £3000 and £10 000, and finally succeeded in reaching the lower figure from a reported 10 000 subscribers.

Herbert Baker, an architect who had helped plan the layout of the Commonwealth's cemeteries in France, advised the committee that the original site on North Terrace was not suitable, so a broader site was sought and granted in the

Pennington Gardens. The designers of the original Cross and
Stone, Mr Blomfield and Sir Edward Lutyens respectively,
gave their permission for the committee to use their designs
for nominal fees, but a setback occurred when the St Peter's
Cathedral authorities announced their intention of raising a
similar cross at the Cathedral's entrance. It was an extraor-
dinary and disconcerting coincidence but after earnest dis-
cussion, and no doubt emotional pleas, the Cathedral agreed
to relocate their cross to the church car park.

Tea Tree Gully stone from the St Peter's College quarry
was chosen and the project was placed in the hands of a local
architect, Sir Alfred Wells. Walter Torode of Unley was
the contractor chosen to carry out the work, and it was to
become a labour of love for him, since, according to the
architect, he ended the project £100 out of pocket. The
foundation stone was laid on 4 August 1920 by the Governor,

Sir Archibald Weigall, and a procession of 1500 women braved miserable weather to place flowers and gifts on the site.

The Cross was officially unveiled on Anzac Day 1922 in conjunction with the returned servicemen's parade, which had been organised to finish at the new memorial. Ten thousand onlookers witnessed the religious service to which the committee had carefully invited ministers from every denomination to escape any charge of sectarian bias. They had hoped to secure the services of the Prime Minister, Mr Hughes, or General John Monash, but had to settle for a local hero, Brigadier General Leane, who took the opportunity to recall the heroism of the original Anzac Day. As a final tribute, a scroll with the names of Adelaide's dead was enclosed within the base of the Cross.

The Anzac Day parade still ends at the Women's War Memorial where, as the last post sounds, memories are awakened of similar cemeteries in the fields of France.

References

Advertiser, 26 April 1922, p 7

Register, 5 August 1920, p 5

Women's War Memorial Committee Minutes, Mortlock Library of South Australiana, PRG 89

WAR HORSE MEMORIAL

Corner of East and North Terraces

Rough hewn granite trough 16 feet (4.9 metres) long raised on a short stone base. A central headstone with inscription 'This trough was erected by public subscription to commemorate the noble services of Australian horses toward the Empire's victories in the Great War'. On the reverse is the Biblical inscription from Job: 'He paweth in the valley, and rejoiceth in his strength. He goeth on to meet the armed men, he mocketh at fear, and is not affrighted, neither turneth his back from the sword.' Unveiled 30 January 1923.

The feats of animals frequently overshadow the deeds of men, and the memorial to the fighting horses of the first world war preceded the one to their riders. The initial suggestion came from the *Register* newspaper and early public subscription raised £248. However, enthusiasm subsequently waned until 1921, when Miss E Abbot, a reporter for the *Register*, and Alec Morrison organised public meetings and secured further funds from the racing clubs.

The organisers chose a beautifully practical monument. The trough is now dry and merely decorative but originally it stood in Victoria Square opposite Grote Street and was connected to the water mains to service the working horses of the Central Market. The horse gradually disappeared from the city centre and when Victoria Square was redesigned in 1964 it was decided to shift the memorial to a more suitable site. The police barracks at Fort Largs and the South Parklands were both suggested but members of the Light Horse Association were keen to have it beside their own memorial in the East Parklands. The monument was resited on 18 April 1967 in time for the Anzac Day commemorations.

The unveiling ceremony was held at the end of a working day when Brigadier-General Raymond Leane, the Police Commissioner, officially turned on the water. Leane was a curious choice since his military roots were firmly with the infantry as Commander of the 'Fighting 48th' battalion. A brother, three nephews and several other relatives filled the ranks and the 48th was commonly known as the 'Joan of Arc' battalion because it was 'made of all Leanes'. In his address Leane also paid tribute to the camel and the mule, both less fashionable than the horse.

The trough was carved in Adelaide by WH Martin of Unley and the proportions and rough finish were intended to symbolise the strength and toughness of the bush horses, or walers, of the Light Horse, which were highly prized in the British Army. In all 39 348 horses were shipped overseas to the Australian Imperial Force, and it is sobering to remember that only one General's horse is reputed to have returned to Australia at the finish of hostilities. All the rest were either sold or destroyed and perhaps it was guilt over their treatment that prompted the desire to enshrine their memory.

References

Advertiser, 31 January 1923, p 9

Adelaide City Council Archives, File No 1146/21

Bean, CEW *Official History of Australia in the War 1914 – 1918*, Angus & Robertson, Sydney, 1936, vol 11, p 543

Nairn, B *Australian Dictionary of Biography*, vol 10, 1986, p 40

SIR SAMUEL WAY

Prince Henry Gardens, beside the Pulteney Street entrance to the University of Adelaide, North Terrace

Life-size bronze statue on a stone plinth. A plaque facing the roadway reads: 'The Right Honourable Sir Samuel James Way. Baronet PC, Lieutenant Governor. Chief Justice. Chancellor of the University of Adelaide. 1836–1916.' Unveiled 17 November 1924.

Sir Samuel James Way was a great man who fully appreciated his own worth. His energy and drive distanced him from his contemporaries and in an era that appreciated hard work and accepted airs and graces he was described as 'the colony's first citizen'. Succeeding generations thought him pompous and forgot his achievements at a pace that would have astounded him, and his attitudes and opinions have now largely fallen out of favour.

Colonial freedom and social mobility had allowed this son of a non-conformist Methodist minister to rise to the position of Chief Justice and to a place in the Privy Council.

Success was measured by social position and Way was ever eager to gather kudos and maintain his role of colonial bene-factor and confidant of royalty.

Way was born on 11 April 1836 in Portsmouth, England. His father embarked on a missionary career in the new colony of South Australia and Samuel followed his family to these shores in 1853. Lack of means had prevented him from continuing his education in England and life in South Australia must have seemed a poor substitute. His first three years in the colony were undecided and hesitant but in 1856 he took articles in a legal firm. The legal profession was

SSL: MB16422

remarkably flexible at this time due to a persistent shortage of lawyers in the colonies. No distinction was made between solicitors and barristers and an 'articled' apprenticeship was sufficient qualification. This freedom, coupled with an obvious talent for the law, allowed Way's meteoric rise in his chosen profession and within 15 years his energy and drive had carried him to the post of Chief Justice. Fortune certainly smiled on him. He acquired a lucrative legal practice when his head of chambers fell ill and his first foray into politics placed him in the position of Attorney-General when the Chief Justice, Sir Richard Hanson, died unexpectedly. As Attorney-General it was Way's duty to recommend a replacement and he unabashedly placed himself at the head of the list. The new position meant a substantial drop in income but, as Way himself surmised, such an opportunity would not come his way again.

Prestige outweighed monetary gain at various stages of Way's career and honours were shrewdly assessed before they were sought or accepted. He repeatedly refused a knighthood because one of his subordinate judges had the higher distinction of KCMG. Way eventually accepted a baronetcy in 1899, a singular honour since only four others then existed in Australia. As Chief Justice he was also de facto Lieutenant-Governor, a position which directly involved him with a succession of distinguished Britons holding the Governorship. Characteristically, Way succeeded in formalising this position so he could be granted the title Lieutenant-Governor.

Way's most meaningful achievements were judicial. His incisive ability and diligence brought him respect and renown within the legal profession and his prodigious capacity for work and leadership helped to create the profession as it exists in the State today. Even the finer details of attire delighted him, and his English tailored gown trimmed with ermine distinguished him at a time when court dress rules were still informal. His appointment to the judicial committee of the Privy Council was a remarkable achievement, since he had effectively joined the highest court of the Empire.

By this time Way had become a grand figure whose departures and arrivals within the state were accompanied by crowds and whose residence, Montefiore in North Adelaide, was virtually an extension of Government House. His popularity was fanned by noble pursuits and philanthropic endeavours which included governorships on the boards of charitable and educational institutions. As the first president of the Adelaide Children's Hospital his name still graces one of the main buildings. Other presidencies held by him included that of the Deaf and Dumb Institution, the Art Gallery and the Museum. He was also Chancellor of the University and Grand Master of the Freemasons. He maintained this prodigious work effort until his death on 8 January 1916. Even while he was succumbing to a form of muscle cancer he continued his duties on the bench after the amputation of an arm. He was given a state funeral and characteristically Sir Samuel Way, South Australia's first citizen, stipulated the route of the procession before he died.

The idea for a memorial statue had also been mooted before Way's death. After refusing earlier offers he had finally agreed to his friend Sir Langdon Bonython's suggestion in 1914. Bonython promptly raised £1600 from 16 friends, and Way kept a confidential list of the subscribers. The choice of sculptor fell automatically on Alfred Drury, whom Way had been instrumental in selecting for Sir Thomas Elder's memorial and whose work, despite exasperating delays, he had warmly applauded. Way had planned to sit for the sculptor but his physical illness overcame his aspirations.

The long delay in completing the statue was mainly due to the wartime shortage of copper. Way was represented standing in his Chief Justice's robes as if caught in mid-discourse. The memorial was unveiled before a large crowd on Monday 17 November 1924 by Sir George Murray, who had succeeded Way to the positions of Lieutenant-Governor, Chief Justice and Chancellor. A lengthy speech was needed to list all Way's achievements and it was reported verbatim in the newspaper the following day.

Despite his many vanities Way's energy and intellect were a great boon to South Australia and all levels of Adelaide society benefited from his interests. However, society was rapidly changing and Sir Samuel Way's efforts were soon lost in the rush. Today Way's statue is easily missed, as it does little to draw the attention of passers-by. The lengthy list of honorifics on the pedestal now seems slightly pompous and perhaps 'leading citizen and philanthropist' would have been more appropriate.

References

Hannan, AJ *The Life of Chief Justice Way*, Adelaide, 1960

Serle, G *Dictionary of Australian Biography*, Angus & Robertson, 1949, p 469

Cyclopedia of South Australia, 1901, p 245

Register, 18 November 1924, p 8

Way, SJ Letters of Sir Samuel Way 1915–1916, Mortlock Library of South Australiana, PRG 630/5

LIGHT HORSE MEMORIAL

**South-eastern corner of the intersection of
East and North Terraces**

Granite obelisk 36 feet (11 metres) high standing on a stepped base on which is recorded the theatres of the first world war in which the Light Horse served: Egypt, Palestine and Gallipoli. The obelisk is surmounted by a light which burns from dusk to dawn. The monument is placed on a small grassy knoll with the parklands falling away behind leaving it prominent against the sky. On the column facing North Terrace is the dedication: 'Australian Light Horse 1914 – 1918. At the Going Down of the Sun We Will Remember Them.' Unveiled 5 April 1925.

In the newly created Australian Federation at the turn of the century, South Australia was designated a 'country state' and many of its country sons served in the Light Horse. The Light Horse regiments, mounted infantry, as distinct from cavalry were an established feature of the Australian militia that had already played a useful role in the Boer war.

The Light Horse took pride in its bush-bred resilience and horsemanship, and at the start of the war men and horses came from all parts of Australia, eventually filling three brigades. However, when the static nature of the conflict in Europe became apparent they were designated a role in the Middle East where their final training had taken place. Dismounted, they played a major role in the second phase of the Gallipoli campaign during the feint attacks of August 1915, but their major contribution to the war was in Egypt and Palestine as part of the Desert Column which continued the war against Turkey. They helped defend Egypt and then gained fame in the advance to Jerusalem by charging the defences of Beersheba. Light Horse casualties never approached the carnage of the Western Front, and on long dusty patrols the greatest enemy for man and horse was the desert itself. The end of this war was also the end of the Light Horse's role in battle, although the romantic image of the plumed riders still causes excitement today.

After the first world war there was a profusion of memorial committees and memorial funds, and the fund raising for the Light Horse monument began in 1919. The committee's president was Dr Charles Duguid, who had been an army surgeon in a Light Horse regiment. Duguid had migrated to Australia in 1911 and after the war he settled in Magill, South Australia. Remembered as one of the founding figures of the Aboriginal mission at Ernabella, he was a champion of Aboriginal causes right up to his death in 1986. No record of the committee's activities appears to have survived but contemporary newspapers reported that the memorial cost £1200, and that most of the funds were donated by friends and relatives of the fallen. The designer of the monument was South African born George Gavin Lawson, who had migrated to Australia in 1912. The choice of a monument styled on those of ancient Egypt is an appropriate reminder that the Australian soldiers fought in the cradle of civilisation.

The committee originally asked for a site adjacent to the gates of the Botanic Gardens but the City Council refused this request and instead offered the parklands site on the north-east corner of the terraces. This fortunate piece of town planning gave the Light Horse Memorial an eye-catching position matched by few other Adelaide memorials.

Lieutenant-General Sir Tom Bridges, the Governor of South Australia from 1922 to 1928, was given the honour of unveiling the monument. This much-wounded warrior was famous for leading two exhausted battalions to safety during the retreat from Mons, using a tin whistle and drum. A troop of returned Light Horsemen formed the honour guard and both pipe and brass bands performed. Since the monument was intended to honour the fallen the ceremony, held on a Sunday, was a memorial service.

The monument's simple design in smooth stone gives it a sense of the eternal, and it should serve its purpose well.

References

Advertiser, 6 April 1925, p 14; 6 December 1986, p 40

Observer, 11 April 1925, p 31

McRae, L *Light Horse*, Brighton, 1986

Journal of Royal Australian Institute of Architects,
    April–June 1953, p 13

SIR ROSS SMITH

Creswell Gardens, at the intersection of
War Memorial Drive and King William Road

Bronze statue dressed in flying coat and helmet standing on a
globe of the world, with one foot resting in Europe and the
other in Australia. Two bronze female figures stand on a
lower level, one holding an aeroplane representing Flight,
and the other, wearing a winged helmet, representing
Intrepidity. Bronze reliefs on all four sides of the plinth depict
brother Keith Smith and events of the historic flight,
including the departure from London with St Paul's in the
background, touchdowns in India and Burma, and the arrival
in Adelaide with the twin towers of the post office and town
hall. Inscriptions on the front and back of the plinth identify
Sir Ross, proudly claim him as a son of Adelaide born at
Semaphore, and commemorate the flight, all the participants
and the make and registration number of the plane. Unveiled
10 December 1927.

The excitement of the early flying age has long faded and the feats of its pioneers have been forgotten. In the age of supersonic jets it is hard to believe the hysteria that greeted the first 28 day flight between England and Australia. Pilots Ross and Keith Smith and their mechanics Shiers and Bennett, gingerly hopping from one makeshift airstrip to the next, were unaware of the increasing public excitement. On touching down in Darwin on 10 December 1919 they were bewildered by the storm of acclaim. It was the beginning of a public love affair with all deeds aeronautical. The acclaim was international and within two weeks of touchdown both pilots were knighted.

The Australian government had sparked the excitement with the offer of £10 000 to the first Australian to fly the distance within 30 days. The aeroplane companies were also eager to support the intrepid pilots who could prove their machines. Navigation and the lack of facilities and supplies en route were major obstacles and both fortune and skill were required. Only one other contestant reached Australian shores and the race proved fatal to others. Ironically, after overcoming the hazards of Europe and Asia the journey from Darwin to Adelaide took over three months.

Ross Smith had all the trappings of the romantic hero. He was educated at Queens College, North Adelaide. His family managed an outback station where he learnt horsemanship and at school he was a horse cadet and a natural leader. The Light Horse seemed the natural arena for his military career and he fought at Gallipoli but the lure of the skies drew him away. In October 1915 he joined the Royal Flying Corps and served in Palestine, and in 1917 he transferred to the Australian Flying Corps. With the derring-do of

'Flight' symbolic figure on Sir Ross Smith memorial

a flying ace he collected decorations and a reputation as one of Australia's best pilots. The support of his superior officers helped him to acquire his Vickers-Vimy aircraft for the fateful race.

Like so many other heroic adventurers, Ross Smith's life ended in tragedy. While preparing for a round-the-world dash with his brother Keith in 1922 his plane fell into a spin during familiarisation trials at Weybridge in England, killing him instantly. The expressions of grief were immediate: the *Register* opened a 'shilling fund' for a memorial and collected £1500 within weeks and the Lord Mayor, Sir Lewis Cohen, called a public meeting to form a memorial committee. The nature of the memorial was the subject of intense debate. One popular suggestion was a memorial tower at Mount Lofty that would double as a navigation beacon when interstate flights eventuated. By September 1923, £4500 had been collected. The memorial committee decided on a statue and announced a competition open to sculptors from England and Australia. Eighteen entries were submitted and first place plus a prize of £200 was awarded to Frederick Brook Hitch, whose design captures the image and deeds of its subject, with a touching reminder that the plane and its crew were equally important.

Ross Smith had advocated the Creswell Gardens as a fitting site for a memorial to the 3rd Light Horse Brigade and this swayed the committee's choice of position for his own memorial. The unveiling was held on a Saturday morning and was well attended. It was the eighth anniversary of the historic flight and pilots and their machines were still astounding the world. In his unveiling speech the Lieutenant-Governor, Sir George Murray, described Sir Ross as the 'state's most famous son'. Three planes circled overhead, droning a mechanical dirge to the fallen hero.

References

Adelaide City Council Archives, File No 1229/22

Register, 8 September 1922, p 6; 13 October 1922, p 6;
    21 September 1923, p 8; 2 December 1924, p 9;
    12 December 1927, p 8

Serle, G *Dictionary of Australian Biography*, vol 2, 1949, p 337

SOUTH AUSTRALIAN NATIONAL WAR MEMORIAL

North-western corner of Kintore Avenue and North Terrace

Stone arch with two recessed sculptural groups on each side raised on a stepped dais. Unveiled 25 April 1931.

The omnipresent war memorials which are to be found in Australia's towns and cities are evidence of the profound effect of the first world war on every community. Australia had suffered its heaviest casualties of any war and so many of the dead lay in unknown graves on foreign shores. The construction of a large state memorial was only a matter of time but as the years passed public impatience grew. Unfortunately, the government's memorial committee could not reach consensus over the site or the style of the monument. As early as 1919 a survey of prominent architects had selected Montefiore Hill as the most suitable site, but eventually the Government House domain was chosen, originally just within the entrance at the south-western corner.

A design competition was announced in 1924 with specifications for a suitable monument. In a mixture of parochialism and Empire unity, the competition was limited to South Australians who were also British subjects. Misfortune intervened when the original 26 entries were completely destroyed by fire but this catastrophe at least enabled the committee's assessors to rethink the site requirements and subsequently select a site on the south-eastern corner of the Government House domain, where the memorial was finally erected. It was not until 1926 that the local architects Woods, Bagot, Jory and Laybourne-Smith were judged the winners for their concept of a rugged canopy of Harcourt granite with inset sculptural groups. The estimated cost was £30 000 on completion and the Sydney sculptor Raynor Hoff was one of the few in Australia who could handle bronzes of this size.

Raynor Hoff was born on the Isle of Man in 1894 and moved to Sydney in 1919 to head the Technical College, where he gradually established an active and acclaimed school of sculpture. The large bronze panels he created for the Dubbo War Memorial in 1925 were among his first major works and he later completed the massive Anzac Memorial in Sydney's Hyde Park. A straightforward and hard living man, his career was plagued by controversy and moral outrage after his depiction of a nude female figure on the Cross of Sacrifice in Sydney. Hoff worked in the classical mould but avoided the common heroic images of war. The tired, crumpled, resigned figures on his Hyde Park memorial were abhorred by many for their despondent realism, and he did not live to see their appreciation by subsequent generations. Suffering poor health due to excessive alcohol consumption,

he was dumped by a wave while surfing and died of pancreatitis at the age of 43 on 19 November 1937.

Hoff did not generally carve stone, preferring to model in clay, and use assistants to transpose to stone. The winged

colossi that fill both recesses of the granite arch of the South
Australian War Memorial were the first to be worked from
Angaston white marble, which has been described as similar
to, but coarser than, the famous Pentelic marble of Athens.
The images are heavily, almost cloyingly, symbolic. The
sculptural group facing North Terrace represents the pro-
logue to war: the student, farmer and girl dropping the
emblems of their lives and offering themselves to the winged
Spirit of Duty, which carries a sword as a cross, symbolising
battle and sacrifice. The reverse side is the passive epilogue:
another Spirit carrying a stricken youth symbolises
Womanhood sacrificing her sons and lovers. The words of
John Oxenham eulogise the lost: 'All honour give to those
who nobly striving nobly fell that we might live.' The con-
stant splash of the fountain beneath is a reminder of the
continuous flow of memories, while the bronze crowned
lion, also sculpted by Hoff, reinforces the imperial theme.

Two entrances lead into the cool, quiet, domed inte-
rior of the memorial where gilt honour rolls list the names of
the fallen under their serving battalions. This is a place of
repose and reflection. The valedictory is inscribed above:
'Their glory survives in everlasting remembrance. Not graven
in stone but enshrined for all time in the hearts of man.'

An estimated 75 000 people attended the unveiling at
noon on 25 April 1931. There was a fitting martial flavour,
with ex-servicemen, scouts, guides, wolf cubs and brownies
forming the honour guard. Other onlookers lined North
Terrace and even clambered over the regal statue of King
Edward VII to gain a vantage point. The memorial was
unveiled by the Governor, Brigadier-General Sir Alexander
Hore-Ruthven, one of the toughest and most resourceful to

have served in this state. Described by his prospective father-in-law, in a remarkable example of poor judgement, as 'the impecunious son of an impoverished family with indifferent prospects'. Hore-Ruthven earned a Victoria Cross in Egypt in 1899 while only attached to the militia and fought and was wounded on the Gallipoli peninsula. He retired from the army in 1928 to become one of a long line of South Australian military governors and proved, during a period of financial strife, social conflict and depression, to be one of the most active and outspoken. In 1935 he became Governor of New South Wales and then as Baron Gowrie, Governor-General of Australia from 1936 up to and throughout the second world war. He was granted on earldom on his retirement in 1945.

Today the War Memorial sits a little incongruously on a busy city corner, unobstructed and open to passers-by during the bustle of the working day. The symbolism is probably lost in our less spiritual society but the frequent splash of colour from wreaths placed for all types of occasions is a pleasing reminder of its enduring significance.

References

Adelaide City Council Archives, File No 2718

Beauchamp, Earl, *Sculpture of Rayner Hoff*,
    Sunnybrook Press, 1984

The Chronicle, 25 April 1931, p 52

Nairn, B *Australian Dictionary of Biography*, Melbourne
    University Press, 1983, p 63; p 327

Scarlett, K *Australian Sculptors*, Thomas Nelson, 1980, p 260

Woods, Bagot, Jory, Laybourne-Smith, Architects,
    National War Memorial Brochure, Adelaide

MATTHEW FLINDERS

Prince Henry Gardens, facing the intersection of
Stephens Place and North Terrace

Life size bronze statue in full naval regalia standing on a
granite plinth decorated with bronze panels, on the western
side showing Flinders's route around Australia and on the
eastern side a map of his explorations of South Australia and
the locations named by him. Unveiled 12 April 1934.

Flinders' prodigious achievements failed to receive the
acclaim they deserved during his lifetime due to personal
misfortunes, especially his years of imprisonment by the
French as a result of the Napoleonic Wars. He died in 1814 a
broken and ignored man, the day after his book, *An Account
of a Voyage to Terra Australis*, which contained charts of virtually all the country's coastline and which popularised the
name Australia, was published. South Australia ceased to be
terra incognita and most of its best known coastal landmarks
were named by Flinders.

Australia was tardy in recognising the achievements of

its famous explorer and only the offer of Flinders's original ship's log to the first city to erect a statue in his honour prompted action. Sydney won the day and the log now resides in the Mitchell Library.

Adelaide's effort failed due to the exigencies of war and public apathy. In 1921 an enthusiastic public meeting set about collecting the estimated £3000 for a statue but this effort soon waned, and it was not until a statue was erected in Melbourne in 1925 that angry letters were written to newspapers and enquiries were made regarding the funds. Money remained the stumbling block, and South Australia's lacklustre effort seemed to epitomise the public and official indifference that had always plagued Matthew Flinders. The secretary of the statue fund was Fred Johns, the virtual founder of Australia's *Who's Who*, and he remained the life and soul of the movement during the doldrums of the 1920s. Johns died in 1932 only two years before the statue's unveiling.

The statue was sculpted and cast in the United Kingdom by Frederick Brook Hitch (1871–1957), who had been acclaimed for his memorial to Sir Ross Smith in 1927. Hitch based the likeness on miniatures and portraits provided by Flinders's grandson, the archaeologist, Sir Flinders Petrie. The uniform is a replica of the period and the sextant and telescope are symbols of Flinders's naval calling. Fittingly, a broken mast was also included as a reminder of his misfortunes, yet far from looking distraught, the explorer's attitude is calm and contemplative as he stands, elbow on arm.

The statue was unveiled by Governor Sir Alexander Hore-Ruthven. As one of his last official acts as governor, he eulogised Flinders's qualities of initiative and enterprise as the

foundation of the British Empire. Ten groups of sea scouts formed the guard of honour and among those attending was Sir Douglas Mawson, another renowned explorer.

Matthew Flinders's statue is almost lost amid the leafy gloom of North Terrace, where it is frequently enveloped by tree branches. His true memorials are the place names all around us, from Mt Lofty to the shore.

References

Adelaide City Council Archives, File No 958/20

Advertiser, 13 April 1934, p 22

The News, 12 April 1934, p 1

Whitington, LA Matthew Flinders and Terra Australis, Pamphlet 1951, Mortlock Library of South Australiana

WAR MEMORIAL CROSSES

**Behind the State War Memorial, on the north-western
corner of Kintore Avenue and North Terrace**

Six canopied alcoves containing battered wooden crosses of
various designs placed at regular intervals along the outer
face of the Government House domain wall. Perspex weather
screens cover the fronts of the alcoves. The original inscriptions are still visible on each cross and plaques placed beside
the alcoves read from North Terrace : 'Tobruk Siege', '10th
Battalion Pozieres', '27th Battalion Pozieres', '48th Battalion,
Pozieres', '50th Battalion, Villers Bretonneux', 'Royal
Australian Regiment, Korea, Malaya, Borneo, Vietnam'. The
first world war crosses unveiled 31 July 1938; Tobruk Siege
cross 19 April 1979; Royal Australian Regiment 18 August
1979.

The first world war battlefields of the Western Front were
household names in Australia in the 1920s and 1930s, etched
in memory by the bitter losses and desperation of the
fighting. Pozieres was a small village in the Somme Valley

which became the scene of Australia's baptism of fire in France in 1916 and where the Australians suffered heavy battle casualties. In 45 days during July and August 1916, the Australian divisions launched nineteen attacks to capture a small ridge, suffering 23 000 casualties. Australia's official war historian sadly describes this ridge as '... more densely sown with Australian sacrifice than any other place on earth.' The slight hill was purchased by the Australian government and a monument now marks the site beside the busy road linking the French cities of Albert and Bapaume.

The 10th, 27th and 48th, all South Australian Battalions, were savaged in the Pozieres fighting. The 48th suffered the heaviest losses, with 25 officers and 610 men killed or injured out of a total of 750. The crosses were made from scrounged wood and erected immediately after the fighting ended, in

August 1916. The 27th's cross was carved by Sergeant R Tehan from a plank of a church door. It was at least 7 feet high (2.1 metres) and lost its lower bar to artillery fire during the German offensive of March 1918. The crosses would have dominated the crushed skyline of the Pozieres battlefield.

Villers Bretonneux, 25 kilometres south-west of Pozieres, is the site of Australia's largest war memorial and cemetery in France. It marks the limit of the German advance in March 1918 and was the scene of the Australian 13th Brigade's night counterattack on 24 April, which recaptured the town and earned enduring fame as one of the most daring achievements of Australian arms.

With the re-organisation of the war graves and construction of stone memorials, the crosses became redundant. The decision to save them was a testament to the emotion and trauma of the fighting. In 1927 the Australian War Memorial received the remains of the three wooden Pozieres crosses and offered them to South Australia. The 27th Battalion originally suggested erecting their cross in Unley from where many of the early recruits had come but the desire to keep them together prevailed. They are powerful symbols of the sorrow felt by comrades in the bleak respite of war and probably meant more to the survivors than the memorial they face.

References

Advertiser, 21 September 1933, p 55; 1 August 1938, p 19

Bean, CEW *Anzac to Amiens*, Angus & Robertson, Canberra, 1946, p 264

PIONEER WOMEN'S MEMORIAL

Between the Parade Grounds and the northern wall of the Government House domain, off King William Road

Rectangular garden of floral beds, shrubs and mature trees with a central aisle leading to a statue of a single female figure standing on a buttressed plinth, all enclosed within a red-bricked wall. The western facing side of the plinth is inscribed with the words 'This garden of remembrance and the flying doctor base at Alice Springs were established in the centenary year 1936'. On the northern side there is a sundial with instructions for use and the words: 'Designed by George F Dodwell Esq Government Astronomer 1941', and on the southern side a bronze book inscribed with the words 'The hours vanish yet are they recorded'. Unveiled 19 April 1941.

The South Australian centenary celebrations in 1936 were a gala community occasion which stimulated a flurry of com-memorative activities. Not surprisingly, pioneer themes pre-dominated and when the government sponsored the South Australian Women's Centenary Council in 1935, a memorial to the hitherto unsung pioneer women was the result. Since the minutes of the memorial committee were sealed in a time capsule within the statue's base, the genesis of the memorial cannot be revealed until 2036. The time capsule also contains messages for the women of the future.

Adelaide Miethke was President of the Women's Centenary Council and chair of the subsequent Pioneer Women's Memorial Trust. Miethke was a pioneer unionist for the Teachers' Association who succeeded in establishing better conditions for female teachers, but little is recorded of her public face or personality. There were four other trustees, including the much admired Dorothy Dolling, who from 1937 wrote the Women's Page of *The Chronicle* under the pen name of Eleanor Barbour. Fund raising began immediately and £6250 was raised quickly. A Book of Remembrance was one novel idea, with women paying one shilling for the privilege of listing their pioneer ancestors. This valuable record was also sealed into the time capsule.

The nature of a fitting memorial to South Australia's pioneer women was much debated in 1936. Practical and functional memorials were popular, in reaction to the profusion of decorative and symbolic memorials erected after the first world war. A 'flying sister base' at Port Augusta was mooted and would have made a fitting tribute, but at the request of the Reverend John Flynn a flying doctor base was funded at Alice Springs instead. This was a bold decision as it placed South Australia's memorial beyond its borders, so the committee resolved to erect a symbolic memorial in the capital as well. A women's pioneer garden, including the sundial and crypt, had been built in Melbourne in 1935 and this provided an example for Adelaide.

In 1938 the committee requested the use of city park-land beside the parade grounds to establish a Garden of Remembrance, which was to be the setting for a commemorative statue. Elsie Cornish, a landscape gardener, became the honorary designer and appears to have done most of the planting. The City Council happily gave its permission but problems arose, first when it was realised that provision for water supply had not been made, and subsequently when councillors complained that the appearance of the garden was the cause of much negative comment. This prompted the City Curator to recommend that the sooner the council took over the better.

Ola Cohn, a Melbourne sculptor, was commissioned to create the memorial. The deliberations relating to this decision are also securely enclosed in the pedestal, but Cohn has recorded that she was asked to submit a design for the memorial in 1938, but on whose recommendation is unknown. At that time Cohn was preoccupied with her dying sister and tried to decline but reported that she 'was up against a committee of lively and energetic women. They wanted a memorial and they wanted me to execute it.' Yet her first three designs were not accepted, and it was only when she braved her first flight to see the garden that she was able to compose a figure to their liking. Remarkably, she modelled a 7 inch (17.7 cm) figure in clay the following day and proposed to carve it freehand from stone.

Cohn was an interesting choice. Born in Bendigo, she was adventurous and outrageously modern in the predominantly traditional art scene of the 1930s. She had determinedly pursued a career in sculpture at a time when it was an unfashionable career for women. After studying at the

Swinburne Technical College in Melbourne, she spent four years at the Royal College of Art in London, where she worked with Henry Moore and wandered the galleries of the British Museum. On returning to Melbourne she mounted the first exhibition of modern sculpture in that city in 1931, to a mostly hostile reaction. No large commissions followed until 1934, when she produced two figures for the portico of the Royal Hobart Hospital which again received savage criticism. This conservative pressure gradually softened the lines and planes of her work and the Pioneer Women's Memorial is a soft, smooth figure, with a realistic, gentle face.

Ola Cohn chose a 3-ton piece of Waikerie limestone that was too large to enter her studio, so it spent 18 months in her courtyard braving all types of weather. Carving her 'lady' became a labour of love and the unveiling was a moment of extreme anxiety and soaring pride for the sculptor. However, she was brought firmly back to earth the following day when even this figure proved controversial. Cohn had deliberately wanted to produce a timeless figure undated by form, dress or style, and in this she has undoubtedly succeeded. She felt compelled to explain her design as 'the spirit of womanhood capable of giving birth to a nation'. The coarse 'unladylike' hands represented 'the power and strength of a symbolic woman'.

The sundial was also a labour of love for George Dodwell, the South Australian Government Astronomer, who manned the West Terrace Observatory which stood, from 1899 until it was demolished in 1952, on the site where the Adelaide High School is located. Dodwell spent six months designing a unique sundial that would accurately record the time on every day of the year, but when the dial was mounted he discovered that it was two minutes out, and he had to complete hurried adjustments. The design, although apparently ancient, appeared modern in its novelty.

The opening ceremony coincided with the opening of the Flying Doctor Base in Alice Springs and in a *tour de force* of technology a radio link was made between the two ceremonies. Adelaide Miethke handed the title deed of the new air base to the president of the Australian Aerial Medical Services, Mr N Taylor, and then presented the garden to the Lord Mayor of Adelaide. Lady Muriel Barclay-Harvey officially unveiled the statue, but when the drapes refused to fall it was Dorothy Dolling who quickly pulled off her white gloves and saved the day.

The garden has now grown into a picturesque haven sheltered by tall trees and with the atmosphere of quiet tranquillity that the designers intended. The towering poplars that nestle and screen the gentle memorial were planted in honour of the five trustees, and on her death in the 1960s, Adelaide Miethke was further honoured by the addition of a stone seat to provide a place of repose. Faithful to its purpose, the garden has become the site for a memorial ceremony to the State's pioneer women, organised by the National Council of Women and held on Australia Day each year.

References

Adelaide City Council Archives, File No 1778/38

Advertiser, 21 April 1941, p 12

Broughton, M *Chronicle Cameos*, Nadjuri Australia, Jamestown, 1977, pp 19–23

Cohn, Ola. Me in the Making, Manuscript, La Trobe Library, Melbourne, pp 429–449

Scarlett, K *Australian Sculptors*, Thomas Nelson, 1980, pp 113–120

KING
GEORGE
V

**Angas Gardens, between McKinnon Parade
and War Memorial Drive**

Larger than life-size bronze equestrian statue of King George V dressed in full field marshal regalia with plumed hat and casually flicking his right hand at his side, raised on an elaborate pedestal. The royal coat of arms frieze is placed on the front of the pedestal, the name 'George V' is carved on the northern face and carved at the rear are the words 'George Frederick Ernest Albert Windsor, born 3 June 1865, ascended the throne 6 May 1910. Died 20 January 1936.' Unveiled 25 April 1950.

King George died on 20 January 1936 after a brief illness. His prominence during the first world war meant that he was much loved and the grief at his death was genuine. The movement to erect a monument in Adelaide began immediately with a public meeting in February; however, for the first time the attempt to erect a royal monument struggled. Popular sentiment may have been high and the statue committee's ambitions grand, but imperial allegiance was shifting in the commercial heartland and moneyed halls of Adelaide.

The statue committee boasted the support of Adelaide's wealthiest man, Lavington Bonython, and it quickly decided on a bold equestrian statue of the martial king, planning to collect a minimum of £5000. The government donated £500 but the statue fund languished despite newspaper appeals, until it became embarrassing to continue the front page call for donations. The paucity of funds, unusual for such a regal undertaking, could perhaps be attributable to competition from other activities planned to mark the centenary celebrations of the settling of South Australia. Whatever the reason, the minimum target was never reached and a reluctant government was left with little option but to make up the difference.

The selection of a sculptor was a stunning example of cultural cringing. Initially all the prominent Australian sculptors, including Rayner Hoff, Paul Mountford, Daphne Mayo and Orlando Dutton were asked to submit designs. However the artist and Victorian gallery owner Daryl Lindsay, when asked to give informal advice, undertook to negotiate with British sculptors. At the fee proffered by the committee Lindsay admitted that few would respond, and indeed only Maurice Lambert, son of the first world war artist George Lambert born in Paris and trained in London, showed any interest. Lambert was a new and exciting sculptor according to the enthusiastic Lindsay, who was particularly impressed with Lambert's eagerness to produce a model. To the chagrin of the newly formed Sculptors Society of Australia, the statue committee refused to conduct a competition and accepted

Lambert's model, despite the fact that it arrived in Adelaide broken.

In the 1930s Lambert was considered an up and coming modern artist and in 1935 hc had just completed decorative panels in the luxury liner *Queen Mary*. Lambert's enthusiasm from the beginning helped to secure him the commission and it was certainly a boon throughout the frustrations and set-backs of the next decade.

A contract was signed for £4000 and Lambert set to work. Unfortunately he had only completed a quarter-size clay model and most of the plaster full-size sculpture when war broke out and he was called up. The clay model was stored in the basement of Australia House for safe keeping, but although the plaster model survived the blitz, by 1945 cracking made it worthless. Lambert estimated that £1800 of the £2000 advance payment had been used and that the work would have to begin again. He offered to return the remaining £200, but the statue committee resolved to proceed, although it had no means of paying. Entreaties to Adelaide's businessmen proved fruitless and the government was forced to pay the additional £2700 required to complete the commission.

Lambert battled to complete the work quickly but with a dearth of trained assistants and low post war priority for use of the foundries the statue was not completed until 1948. Shipping was slow, and finally the work languished at Port Adelaide because of the difficulty of moving it under the tramway wires.

Deciding where to put the statue was proving just as vexatious. From the outset Lambert had indicated that his work should be placed amid the bustling crowd where people could interact with it. How it came to be placed away from the main thoroughfares, isolated and screened from view, is an example of exaggerated and misplaced symbolism. After prolonged bickering over a suitable site it was suggested that alignment with the memorial gardens would 'symbolise and emphasise the Christian Fellowship of the Imperial Crown with the Cross'. An explanatory plaque was to be attached to the pedestal, but the impecunious fund could not afford it, so the rare viewer who happens to stumble upon the statue is left to guess the reason why the late King has been banished to the back blocks.

Since the unveiling took place on Anzac Day following the commemorative ceremony at the Women's Memorial Cross, the crowd was large but the ceremony was low key. The Governor, Sir Willoughby Norrie, made a short speech in praise of the King, followed by a minute's silence in his memory.

King George V was the last monarch to be memorialised in bronze and it is unlikely that there will be another. Lambert had hoped to make an equestrian monument equal to Verrochio's famous work in Venice of the bandit general, Colleoni. He did create an impressive statue but it is placed in an unremarkable site. Good King George's regal forebears hold pride of place in the city but the impetus to erect a monument to him was a pallid reflection of the fervour which led to the creaton of earlier memorials. The decision makers and gentry of Adelaide were becoming less willing to fund symbols of loyalty.

References

King George V Statue Committee, Minutes and Letters, Mortlock Library of South Australiana, SRG 27

Thornton, R 'King George V', *South Australiana*, September, 1983, p 138

Scarlett, K *Australian Sculptors*, Thomas Nelson, 1980, p 348

AUSTRALIAN
AMERICAN
GATEWAY

Botanic Gardens, 200 metres east of the entrance,
North Terrace

Two pillar posts of a gateway beside an ornamental lake. Each post is crowned by a stone globe with gold embossing, one highlighting Australia and the other the United States. The plaque on the northern post is inscribed 'Erected by the Australian American Association in South Australia' and the plaque on the southern post is inscribed: 'In deep gratitude to the men and women of the United States of America who joined in the defence of Australia during the war of 1939–1945.' Unveiled 3 July 1953.

The ornamental memorial gateway sits within an amphitheatre of vegetation in a quiet calm corner of the Botanic Gardens, as enigmatic as any gate that leads nowhere. The records of the South Australian Branch of the Australian American Association from this period are currently missing, so why a gate was chosen for the memorial is for the present time a mystery. Pro-American enthusiasm was high in this country after the second world war, and the Australian American Association in each State organised an appeal to the public to erect a large memorial in Canberra, which stands today as one of the tallest structures on the Canberra skyline. The appeal was so popular that it was oversubscribed, so a local memorial was also planned.

The memorial was unveiled by the Governor, Sir Robert George, with an impressive array of guests, including federal and state parliamentarians, heads of the services in South Australia and heads of the US services in Australia, who flew from Melbourne. The Governor's address reflected the uncertainty of the Cold War era when, once again, Australians and Americans were fighting alongside each other, this time in Korea. He was confident that 'if the tide of history again becomes menacing, the English-speaking democracies will again stand together in the hour of need'.

References

Advertiser, 4 July 1953, p 3

ALICE IN WONDERLAND

North-western corner of Rymill Park, East Terrace

Life-size bronze statue of an animated Alice in the act of turning as if startled by noise, tensed and poised, standing on a circular pedestal surrounded by a garden bed. A circular frieze around the base of the statue depicts figures tumbling over and crowding each other, including the White Rabbit, Tweedledum and Tweedledee and an evil looking Cheshire Cat. On the concrete pedestal are the words: ' "Alice" For the children from Josephine and Norman Lewis.' Unveiled 18 December 1962.

The statue of Alice is one of Adelaide's surprises, perched on a grassy slope in the eastern parklands. The figure has been portrayed realistically by sculptor John Dowie and the lively pose brings the fey spirit to life. She was inspired by the ageless Peter Pan in Kensington Gardens, London, and indeed the Lewis's original intention, expressed in a letter to the City Council in 1960, was to provide a copy of Frampton's famous statue. The opportunity arose in 1960 when the council was redeveloping the eastern parklands and establishing the boat lake, kiosk and facilities. Beautification included gardens and the impish Piccaninny Fountain by Dowie, which stands on the eastern edge of the park.

Adelaide abounds with Dowie's work and he is undoubtedly the city's best known sculptor. Born in 1915, he was educated at Adelaide High School and diverted from a career in architecture by the second world war. While serving in North Africa he was seconded to work with the sculptor Lyndon Dadswell preparing works for the military history

section, and after the war he studied in London and Florence. By 1962 he had become a full time painter and sculptor. His work achieves more than careful representation, it captures appearance and mood in a distinctively impressionistic style. Most of the famous faces along North Terrace have been sculpted by Dowie and his exuberant style can be seen in the fountains of Victoria Square and Veale Gardens. Although in his eighties, he still exhibits his work regularly.

John Dowie recalls that the City of Adelaide Town Clerk, William Veale, was the prime instigator of the beauti-fication of Adelaide's parklands and he actively solicited donations from friends and local businessmen. When Norman Lewis, a successful businessman and the founder and deputy chairman of Beneficial Finance Corporation, offered £1000, the commission was given immediately to Dowie, who estimated that it would probably cost more but discovered that casting in Italy was considerably cheaper than in the UK. How the theme evolved from Peter Pan to Alice in Wonderland is uncertain, but Norman Lewis's son can remember another Alice in a Liverpool park close to where the family resided for a time. The figure was finished and cast within two years, in time for Christmas. It added sig-nificantly to the ornamentation of the city before the opening of Adelaide's first Festival of Arts.

References
Adelaide City Council Archives, File No 411V

Advertiser, 18 December 1962, p 3; 23 October 1965, p 25;
    30 July 1983, p 2

Genders, G 'The Art of John Dowie', in *South Australian Scrapbook*, ed. M. Brunato, Rigby, Adelaide, 1979

VICTOR RICHARDSON GATES

Eastern entrance to Adelaide Oval, off King William Road

Five iron gates framed by iron pylons. A large bronze plaque on the central gate bears the valediction: 'These gates were erected to honour Victor York Richardson 1894–1969. For outstanding services to South Australia in the field of sport', followed by a long list of his sporting achievements, including the captaincy of local, state and national teams. Bronze relief sculptures flank the central gate, on the southern side depicting football, and on the northern side cricket. Unveiled 28 October 1967.

In the 1960s Victor Richardson, one of South Australia's favourite sporting sons of the 1920s and 30s, received the singular honour of commemoration within his lifetime. He had become a grand old man of sporting commentary and coaching and was the stately doyen of the sporting establishment.

In the 1920s amateurism reigned supreme, while professionalism was considered lowbrow and uncouth. Victor

Richardson reached his sporting prime in this period. He was the perfect participant: during a weekend he would play a succession of sports, including, depending on the season, gymnastics, basketball, lacrosse, baseball, tennis, Australian rules football and cricket. He achieved highest acclaim in the last two, captaining his local club Sturt, the State football side in the 1920s, the State cricket side from 1921 to 1935, and the Australian cricket team in overseas tours to New Zealand and South Africa. His Test cricket career was dogged and determined rather than brilliant, which meant that he never achieved the same nation wide celebrity as he did in his home State. However, he subsequently maintained a high sporting profile as a cricket commentator for the ABC, and assisted cricket coaching in schools. He was awarded an OBE in 1954.

The *Advertiser* reported that the Lord Mayor, James Irwin, initiated the movement to honour Richardson and a commemoration committee was formed. The public appeal was supported by the South Australian Cricket Association and the South Australian National Football League, and commemorative gates were chosen as a suitable tribute. The bronze reliefs were added when over £5000 was raised. A local architect, Ian Hannaford, supervised the design and construction and John Dowie designed the friezes with flowing energetic figures. Richardson's features are to be clearly seen facing up at the crease.

The opening ceremony was held during the lunch break at a Sheffield Shield game and the players formed an honour guard. Amongst them were Richardson's two grandsons, Ian and Greg Chappell. Richardson's illustrious contemporary, and president of the SACA, Sir Donald Bradman, gave the address and Richardson responded by ruefully reminding commentators that the description 'memorial gates' was premature. The central plaque was added after his death two years later, giving a detailed listing of his sporting career, as if in testament to the fleeting nature of sporting fame.

References

Adelaide City Council Archives, File No 2827/65

Serle, G *Australian Dictionary of Biography*, vol 11, 1988, p 385

Advertiser, 11 January 1966, p 3; 30 October 1967, p 3

L O R D
F L O R E Y

**Prince Henry Gardens, between King William Street
and Kintore Avenue on North Terrace**

Bronze bust mounted on a small stone obelisk. Under the
bust is a bronze plaque with the name 'Lord Florey' carved in
relief. At the foot of the pedestal on a Harcourt granite base is
a larger bronze plaque with the full title 'The Right
Honourable Howard Walter, Baron Florey of Adelaide and
Marston', followed by a detailed biographical history.
Unveiled 25 June 1969.

A biography is an unusual addition to any commemorative
bust in Adelaide. Perhaps it is a reflection of Florey's per-
plexing obscurity, even in the city of his birth. On the plaque
the biographer has recorded Florey's many achievements
including that he 'showed the curative properties of penicillin
and made it universally available'. The serendipitous discovery of penicillin by Alexander Fleming in 1929 is well
known and has been popularised by its drama and human
interest, yet few would realise that the famous mould then lay

ignored and untouched for almost ten years until fortune intervened again and sparked the interest of Ernst Chain, the key biochemist in Florey's team. This time the therapeutic possibilities did not pass unnoticed and Florey, the unflappable researcher, overcame the problems of the production, purification and vigorous testing of penicillin. His dramatic success against the background of the Battle of Britain and government inertia, surpasses the melodrama of the discovery. The Nobel Prize for Medicine was granted to Fleming, Chain and Florey in 1945.

Born in the Adelaide suburb of Malvern, Florey spent his childhood in Mitcham at the family home, 'Coreega', located on Fullarton Road in Springfield opposite St Michaels Church. A Rhodes scholarship led him to England and a research career which eventually placed him in the Chair of Pathology at Oxford in 1935. He scaled the scientific heights in England, gathering titles and honours culminating in 1965 with a life peerage comprised of Adelaide, his childhood home, and Marston, a small village on the outskirts of Oxford where he had built a small house. Australia was never able to reclaim Howard Florey and his appointment as Chancellor of the Australian National University in 1963, a post he held until his death at age 69 from a heart attack on 21 February 1968, was purely ceremonial.

The bronze bust, in the expressive style of John Dowie, was unveiled on a Wednesday morning in a modest ceremony attended by a few shoppers and office workers and, one suspects, a sprinkling of scientists and doctors from the nearby Royal Adelaide Hospital.

References

Advertiser, 26 June 1969, p 3

Chinner, C *Mitcham Village Sketchbook*, Rigby, Adelaide, 1974

Macfarlane, G *Howard Florey – The Making of a Great Scientist*, London, 1979

SIR
MELLIS
NAPIER

**Prince Henry Gardens, adjacent to the entrance of
Government House, North Terrace**

Bronze bust, on a stone pedestal with two plaques below
listing decorations and titles. Unveiled 2 July 1970.

Sir Mellis Napier's bust faces the busy intersection of King
William Street and North Terrace with an anxious expression. The sculpture was completed in his 88th year, when
he was puzzled and uncertain about the future of the society
he had served for 70 years. His unease is understandable,
since his lifetime spanned the late Victorian era to the tur-
bulent sixties.

John Mellis Napier was born in Dunbar, Scotland, and
emigrated with his family at the age of 16. He received his
legal education at the University of Adelaide and he completed his articles with no less a person than Charles
Cameron Kingston. By age 21 he was the youngest practitioner in the Supreme Court, and it was a steady progression
to King's Council, Supreme Court Justice and Chief Justice in

1942. In 1943 he was knighted, and a KCMG followed in 1948. As Chief Justice for 25 years Napier had a strong influence on the practice of law in South Australia and chaired

some of the more celebrated royal commissions. He regarded law as 'the cement that holds a society together', but realised 'the necessity for its adapting itself to the needs of the community at large'.

The bust was presented to the Corporation of the City of Adelaide by a group of admirers, the chief being Sir Lloyd Dumas, the Chairman and Managing Director of the *Advertiser*. One of Australia's leading newspaper magnates, Sir Lloyd was a man with eclectic interests and an old fashioned feeling of responsibility to the community. His strong support of the first Adelaide Festival of Arts helped to ensure its success. The Adelaide sculptor, John Dowie, had displayed a plaster cast of the bust, valued at $1000, at the 1970 Advertiser Art Exhibition. The City Council subsequently commissioned the pedestal and plaques and, at the suggestion of Sir Lloyd, placed the memorial near the entrance to Government House in recognition of Sir Mellis Napier's long service as Lieutenant-Governor.

The bust was unveiled by the Governor-General, Sir Paul Hasluck, before a crowd of 150 onlookers. Sir Mellis Napier responded to the address, airing his fears regarding the unrest of the current era and his desire to live on 'in the hope of a better time to come'. He died on 22 March 1976 at the age of 93 and was given a State funeral by the society he had served for so long.

References

Adelaide Law Review Association, June 1967

Advertiser, 26 June 1970, p 3; 3 July 1970, pp 2–3;
    23 March 1976, p 5

**Prince Henry Gardens, near the entrance to
Government House, North Terrace**

Bronze bust on a stone pedestal on which a round plaque lists
titles and a lower rectangular plaque provides biographical
details. Unveiled 2 March 1978.

Sir Mark Oliphant was the first South Australian born
Governor and the only royal representative whose features
grace our streets. He is remembered as the people's Governor.
While far from the archetypal conservative, but rather a free
thinker, his outspoken and often controversial statements
were nevertheless well attuned to the conservative heart of
Adelaide. Born on 8 November 1901, he spent his youth in
Mitcham. His penchant for the sciences earned him a cadet-
ship in physics in 1919 and the chance to complete his university education with an honours degree in science in 1922.

The best opportunities were found overseas in this era
and a post-graduate research scholarship carried him to
Cambridge and the Cavendish laboratories, where new

insights into sub-atomic physics and Nobel laureates were then being generated. Physics was an exciting field in the early part of the century. New discoveries and new methods of experimentation attracted graduates and Oliphant's skill with experimental equipment determined the direction of his life. Under the pressure of war new technology was forced into military gadgetry and this eventually brought Oliphant to Los Alamos and a fringe role in the splitting of the atom.

Sir Mark is a thinker and a man of conscience. His anti-Vietnam war stance placed him among the radicals but he was radical only in saying what he thought, without fear or favour. His appointment to the position of Governor brought him out of retirement at the age of 70 and he proved himself to be conscientious in the role as well as a traditionalist when it came to pomp and ceremony. However, he departed from tradition with his forays into political issues, often to the chagrin of the government that had selected him. Although occasionally poorly conceived and interfering, his involvement and comments were usually popular with the media and the general public.

The bust was sponsored by the City Council and was unveiled by the Governor-General, Sir Zelman Cowen, before a crowd of about 100 onlookers. Sir Mark was unable to attend because of illness but in a humble letter he indicated that he was proud to be beside such luminaries as Sir Mellis Napier and Lord Florey.

The sculptor John Dowie has portrayed Oliphant with an upward gaze and a pugnacious jutting jaw. Sir Mark was well pleased with the result and praised Dowie, with whom he had spent 'many memorable hours sitting'.

References

Adelaide City Council Minutes, 12 September 1977

Advertiser, 3 March 1978, p 3

Cockburn, S *Oliphant*, Axiom, Adelaide, 1981

SIR DOUGLAS MAWSON

In front of Bonython Hall, North Terrace

Bronze bust mounted on a marble stand on which Mawson's name, title and qualifications are carved including the description 'Professor of Geology and Mineralogy Antarctic Scientist and Explorer'. A plaque at the base records that the memorial was erected by public subscription. Two boulders flank the stand. On the eastern flank is a pegamite boulder from the Mawson Valley, Arkaroola and on the western a Charnockite boulder from the Mawson Base in Antarctica. Unveiled 16 August 1982.

Sir Douglas Mawson is principally remembered for his exploits in the 'heroic' age of Antarctic exploration, yet far from seeking fame by recklessly dashing across the ice, his aim was the scientific exploration of our Antarctic doorstep. The banner of science also led to his equally extensive investigation of the Australian hinterland. This memorial, with its geological markers from both fields of endeavour, celebrates the centenary of his birth in distant Yorkshire in 1882.

Mawson's family emigrated in 1884 from England to Sydney, where he was educated. It was Adelaide's good fortune to offer him a lectureship in mineralogy and petrology in 1905, and so began his long association with South Australia. Perhaps it was his fascination with glaciation in the Flinders Ranges that kept him within South Australia; it was certainly his desire to see living glaciers in the Antarctic that prompted him to offer his services to the Shackleton expedition of 1909. But science was only an afterthought for Ernest Shackleton, whose chief aim was to reach the Pole. Mawson proved himself a strong and resourceful figure when he achieved the honour of being among the first three to reach the South Magnetic Pole. Despite this honour, Mawson recognised that the real work in the Antarctic was left undone and he turned down an offer to join Scott in his quest for the Pole, in favour of planning a detailed scientific survey of the frozen continent south of Australia.

The Australasian Antarctic Expedition of 1911 began the tradition of Antarctic exploration which continues to this day. The biological, geological, meteorological and magnetic surveys of Mawson's expedition produced more scientific information than the combined efforts of all the other Antarctic expeditions of the era. It also produced one of the epic stories of Antarctic survival as Mawson trekked 100 miles, alone and starving, after his companions had met their deaths.

Mawson returned to the Antarctic in 1929 and 1930 leading the British, Australian and New Zealand Antarctic Research Expedition during which a formal territorial claim was staked. He was to remain the doyen of later Antarctic activity which resulted in permanent Australian bases on the continent, and he was an early conservationist calling for the control of whaling in the seas he knew so well.

The Fourth International Symposium on Antarctic Earth Sciences was brought forward two years and held in Adelaide to mark the centenary of Sir Douglas Mawson's birth. The erection of a bust commemorating Mawson was suggested in 1981 by Dr Fred Jacka of the Mawson Institute and was readily taken up by the City Council, whose Lord Mayor, Dr Jim Watson, launched a public appeal for $9000. John Dowie was the obvious choice as sculptor, since four of his busts already graced the North Terrace gardens. The unveiling was part of the opening ceremonies for the Symposium. Dr Watson made the presentation and called upon Sir Mark Oliphant to unveil the memorial, which he described as a good likeness of his former friend.

Mawson is the eponym of numerous man-made and natural features on two continents and this simple memorial seems hardly adequate for the man who pushed back the frontiers of Australia by millions of years and thousands of miles.

References
Advertiser, 17 August 1982

Adelaide City Council Minutes 1981/82 p 427, pp 566–567

Nairn, B *Australian Dictionary of Biography*, vol 101986, p 454

CATHERINE HELEN SPENCE

South-west corner of Light Square

Life-size bronze statue dressed in severe Victorian costume, with broad shoulders and a serious expression, holding an open book, standing on a 3-tiered triangular pedestal. A bronze plaque at the base of the pedestal is inscribed with the words 'Catherine Helen Spence 1825–1910 social and political reformer, writer and preacher who worked for children'. Unveiled 10 March 1986.

Catherine Helen Spence was a heroine of the 19th century, which makes it remarkable that, towards the end of the 20th century, she should be the recipient of Adelaide's last full figure bronze statue. It was the rediscovery of South Australia's history during its sesquicentenary that prompted the Jubilee 150 Committee to begin to redress the gender imbalance of Adelaide's public memorials by raising a statue to this 'great dame' of Australian politics.

Spence was the towering female personality of her time because of her very public face. She was a social commentator and political reformer who found a voice first through her novels and later as a journalist, gradually developing the confidence to address public meetings and rallies with great force. Hers was a rare female voice in the male dominated colonial society, and her high morals and self-sacrificing philanthropy made her a respected and dignified figure, not easily brushed aside. She was an early migrant to South Australia, which added to her prestige.

Spence's family arrived in Adelaide in 1839 after their fortunes had failed in Scotland. Spence was only 14 and her autobiography paints a forlorn picture of a young girl, just off the ship, sitting on a log in Light Square and 'having a good cry'. Her opportunity for higher education had ended when the family left Scotland, and she was forced to work as a governess, while pursuing her passion to be a writer. Her first novel, *Clara Morrison*, published in 1854, painted a precise picture of colonial life. She produced five more novels, each brimming with social morality and awareness.

Social welfare and political reform were Spence's passion and were pursued in both theory and practice. On the practical level she was a lay preacher, cared for orphans in her own home and was a major organiser for the South Australian Boarding Out Society, which attempted to give orphans a family life. However, she probably devoted her greatest energy to the theory of political reform. Her name is bequeathed to the 'Hare-Spence' system of proportional representation which operates in Tasmania. She stormed the country, and even travelled overseas, lecturing and trying to introduce constitutional change, believing that proportional representation was the only means of ensuring a democratic voice for minorities. She feared the tyranny of the majority, which the developing party political machines threatened to produce. Although she holds the distinction of being the first woman to stand for federal parliament she failed to win

a seat and her efforts to influence the federal conventions were largely unsuccessful. While she pursued legal reform in many areas, including property rights for women and fairer marriage and divorce laws, she was a late supporter of female suffrage and did not join the league until 1891, when, as deputy chairman, her prestige was a major boost to the suffrage cause.

In belated recognition, the Women's Executive Committee of the Jubilee 150 Board embarked on a mission to raise a memorial to this remarkable woman.With an expressed preference for a female artist, a panel of three, Joy Harbison, Heather Bonnin and Kay Hannaford interviewed seven sculptors. They asked three to submit models and selected Ieva Pocius, who had migrated from Lithuania in 1951 at the age of 28. Pocius had studied sculpture at the South Australian School of Art and, although she had little public recognition, her work had been acquired by the Art Gallery of South Australia. Her model of Spence was very simple when compared with the fussy depictions of the other finalists. Pocius wrote that she interpreted Spence's character as 'dynamic, not interested in fashion or outer appearance … a doer, not a philosopher', and had therefore chosen an 'active pose, twisted to make the figure more interesting, with her fingers just opening a book'. Even the triangular pedestal was intended to symbolise dynamism.

It is interesting to note the financial outlay for this contemporary, and relatively simple statue. The sculptor quoted $3500,the stonemasons $2760 and the bronze casters $16 000. The Jubilee 150 Board had budgeted funds for the entire statue but roughly half was raised by an appeal which opened in 1985.

In keeping with the all-women theme, the Queen officially unveiled the statue in a short ceremony as part of her official duties for the state's sesquicentenary. Light Square, which featured so prominently in her self-described moment of despair, is a fitting place for Catherine Helen Spence's statue but it is lost to public view in this little-frequented part of the city. Spence herself would have chosen a bolder position along the boulevards of the city's heart.

References

Thomson, H *Catherine Helen Spence*, University of Queensland Press, St Lucia, 1987

Jones, H *In Her Own Name*, Wakefield Press, Adelaide, 1986

Walker, R 'Catherine Helen Spence and South Australian Politics', *The Australian Journal of Politics and History*, vol 15, no 1, April 1969, pp 35–46

Scarlett, K *Australian Sculptors*, Thomas Nelson, Melbourne, 1980, p 531

Memorial Appeal Sub-committee, Mortlock Library of South Australiana SRG 477

M A R Y

L E E

Prince Henry Gardens on the corner of
King William Street and North Terrace

Bronze bust in realistic style, with sharp features and hair
pulled tightly back and covered with a small frilly hat,
mounted on a pedestal on which there is a plaque bearing the
words 'Mary Lee 1821 – 1909'. A lower plaque lists the following positions 'Secretary and leader of the Women's
Suffrage League 1888 – 1895. Founding secretary of the
Working Women's Trades Union 1890 – 1892. First Official
Visitor to the Lunatic Asylums' and includes the quote 'My
aim is to leave the world better for women than I found it'.
Unveiled 18 December 1994.

Mary Lee migrated to Adelaide in 1879 at the age of 58 to
nurse a sick son, who died shortly after her arrival. Little is
known of her background. Fickle fate brought her to South
Australia, widowed and with one daughter to accompany
her, but she stayed to become the community's most effective
campaigner for women's suffrage. She was an educated,

passionate worker for social justice who saw women's suffrage as an important step to righting the injustices of a society where women were second class citizens with few legal rights and poor wages.

In an era when it was socially unacceptable for women to be vocal, Mary Lee boldly campaigned through letters to newspapers and public meetings. Seven suffrage bills were brought before parliament from 1886, and the Women's Suffrage League was instrumental in organising petitions, including a 'monster' petition in 1894, 122 metres long and with over 11 000 names, which has now been preserved as an important item of the State's political history. An Act introducing full female suffrage was passed on 18 December 1894, making South Australia the first State to give women the vote and one of the first universal democracies in the world.

It was the centenary of this tumultuous vote in the House of Assembly that prompted the erection of a bust to the long forgotten Mary Lee and its unveiling capped a year of celebrations organised by the Women's Suffrage Steering Committee. The Committee's chairperson, Mary Beasley, paid tribute to Mary Lee before a crowd of 150.

Pat Moseley is a relatively new South Australian sculptor with a fresh open enthusiasm for the medium. At a dinner to raise funds to refurbish the broken headstone at Mary Lee's Walkerville grave, Moseley's model impressed the Committee and a decision was made to place a bust along North Terrace. The bronze casting had to be rushed through in six weeks and at the unveiling it sat precariously unfastened on its pedestal.

Mary Lee was not a wealthy woman and her position on the Suffrage League was honorary. Her final years were impoverished but she was proud of her achievement, and her title as 'Honorary Secretary of the Women's Suffrage League' was carved on her headstone. Her bust stares toward Parliament House, a belated recognition of the grass roots idealism and determination that is the soul of a people's democracy.

References

Advertiser, 19 December 1994, p 5

Mansutti, E *Let Her Name be Honoured*, Adelaide, 1994

Nairn, B *Australian Dictionary of Biography*, Melbourne
    University Press, vol 10, 1986, p 50

NAVAL MEMORIAL GARDEN

In the Parklands abutting Sir Edwin Smith Avenue

Garden beds in the shape of an anchor with 32 bronze plaques, commemorating various ships and services, placed beside the curved flukes of the anchor design. A flagpole heads the garden and in front of this lies a restored tombstone placed on a base and back piece of South Australian granite. The inscription on the stone reads: 'Sacred to the memory of Phineas Philip Davies AB HMCS *Protector*. Killed by premature explosion of a cartridge when firing the salute at Glenelg Commemoration Day 28 December 1885.' A dedicatory plaque, at the base of the stone reads 'This tombstone marked the site of the grave of Phineas Davies in Cheltenham Cemetery. Installed as the headpiece of South Australian Naval Memorial when the garden was relocated April 1995.' At the base of the anchor design is a large, modern, two fluked anchor. Unveiled 8 April 1995.

Phineas Philip Davies was the first serving South Australian seaman to die in the colonial navy. A shot fired in celebration

of the colony's foundation claimed his life. As gunner on South Australia's sole naval ship *Protector* he failed to sponge and extinguish the flames in the breech of number five gun causing the blank cartridge to explode as he loaded it. Davies caught the full force of the blast, and another seaman, Daniel Can, was scorched on one side of his body. It was the *Protector*'s first opportunity to fire the royal salute at a Commemoration Day, and the celebrating crowds were left in uneasy speculation when she suddenly lowered her colours and steamed toward Port Adelaide. Can was transferred to a Semaphore hospital and Davies was buried the next day after an on-board coronial inquest.

Davies had no family in South Australia and it was his ship mates who raised the money for his tombstone. He was buried at Cheltenham although subsequently it was discovered that he was Jewish. However his grave site was undisturbed for one hundred years when the stone from the expired plot was offered to the Naval Association. It was taken to HMAS Encounter at Birkenhead, where the original memorial gardens had only just been established.

The Birkenhead memorial had been established in 1986 after the Corvette Association had offered funds surplus to their successful reunion in South Australia. Other naval services and ship associations also dedicated plaques, but the decision to close the Birkenhead depot meant that the memorial garden had to find a new base. Other sites in Port Adelaide were suggested but the Adelaide City Council agreed to provide a site and help establish the garden in the Parklands close to the Women's War Memorial. The Naval Association committee developed the anchor design, and the Navy funded the project. *Courage* roses are to fill the garden beds, and space is available for further plaques.

A crowd of one thousand attended the unveiling which surprisingly failed to attract any media representatives. The garden now forms a focus for past and present Navy personnel, friends and relatives, convenient to the Anzac day ceremonies which end at the Women's Memorial. A Navy Week celebration is also held in the garden on the Sunday closest to 4 October, which marks the day the first Australian naval fleet sailed through Sydney Heads.

References

Register, 29 December 1885, p 6

Raynor, Mary Secretary Memorial Sub Committee, personal communication, August 1995

INDEX

ALSO BY WAKEFIELD PRESS

ADELAIDE'S ARCHITECTURE AND ART

A Walking Guide

Compiled by Michael Queale and Nicolette Di Lernia

Adelaide's Architecture and Art gives you a guided tour of Australia's most gracious city. Six walks take you around the city's precincts, from the fine cultural and institutional areas, through the city's commercial heart, on to the grandeur of nineteenth century residential Adelaide and in to the zones devoted to eating, nightlife and pleasure.

The walks showcase over 320 works of architecture and public art, with notes on the style, history and significance of each item.

ISBN 1 86254 376 3   RRP $22.95

ALSO BY WAKEFIELD PRESS

AFTER LIGHT

A History of the City of Adelaide
and its Council, 1878–1928

Peter Morton

'. . . a superb book, full of wonderful anecdotes and stunning photographs.' – *Advertiser*

'. . . a lucid and witty writer . . . *After Light* is the the bold, but not brutal, wine from his treading of archival grapes.' – Derek Whitelock

After Light is the first scholarly history of the City of Adelaide to appear since 1878. Illustrated with photographs from the invaluable City of Adelaide Archives, the Mortlock Library, and various interstate and British sources, *After Light* aims to entertain as well as inform. To this end, there are plenty of personality studies, human interest stories, and, occasionally, scandal. *After Light* will appeal to everyone who wishes to know more about the City of Adelaide in the early modern period.

ISBN 1 86254 338 0   RRP $34.95

Wakefield Press has been publishing good Australian
books for over fifty years. For a catalogue of current
and forthcoming titles, or to add your name to our
mailing list, send your name and address to
Wakefield Press, Box 2266, Kent Town, South Australia 5071.

TELEPHONE (08) 8362 8800   FAX (08) 8362 7592

Wakefield Press thanks Wirra Wirra Vineyards and
Arts South Australia for their support.